THE BOOK OF FESTIVAL HOLIDAYS

Books by Marguerite Ickis

THE BOOK OF CHRISTMAS
THE BOOK OF FESTIVAL HOLIDAYS
THE BOOK OF PATRIOTIC HOLIDAYS
HANDICRAFTS AND HOBBIES FOR RECREATION AND RETIREMENT
STANDARD BOOK OF QUILT MAKING AND COLLECTING

The Book of FESTIVAL HOLIDAYS

Marguerite Ickis

With drawings by Miriam F. Fabbri

DODD, MEAD & COMPANY NEW YORK

Library of Congress Catalog Card Number: 64-22675
Printed in the United States of America

TO VIRGINIA MUSSELMAN

My Friend at the National Recreation Association

CONTENTS

THE BOOK OF FESTIVAL HOLIDAYS

1. FESTIVAL HOLIDAYS

From St. John's steeple,
I call the people,
On holy days,
To prayer and praise.

INSCRIPTION ON AN OLD BELL—ST. JOHN'S PARISH, PORTSMOUTH

Every civilization has its festivals—be they religious, seasonal or national. Although festivals may vary from country to country in name and manner of observance, in spirit they are always the same joyous occasions.

A festival is the gathering together of people in a community to celebrate a holy or secular holiday. These days that are set aside from all other days on the year's calendar have come to mean a period of relaxation and a measure of freedom from work. The celebrations in general include a procession, rituals, feasts, dancing, singing and much merriment.

Festivals are but one of the many common forces that unite nations and give continuity to cultural thought. They have always been an outstanding expression of man—a common heritage of fear, thanksgiving, joy and devotion. Many customs still practiced today had their origin with pagans who worshiped objects and events they could not understand. These ancient people bowed to the sun because it gave them light and warmth; and the moon, earth, trees and sea were all gods to be appeased and adored. The harvest festival, especially, stems from the pagan custom of offering the first grain and fruits to the gods.

As holiday customs developed, many symbols have come to be associated with them, their origin and significance having been forgotten. Such rites as serving ceremonial cakes, lighting of candles, singing carols, burning bonfires, etc., represent a curious blending of Christian and pagan survivals, and have been variously interpreted in each country. American customs are closely identified with those of England because of our close associations in life of the past.

Festivals play an important role in American culture—they offer an opportunity to search out disappearing immigrant customs that peoples have brought with them in the nature of celebration fun. They offer a wonderful opportunity for self-expression and communication with others through speech, music, pantomime, acting, play and dance. Besides, they are a means of reviving and preserving folk music and dancing, singing games and classic literature from all over the world.

This book tells how American festivals originated and are observed today. The text covers the main Christian and Jewish holy days and secular holidays and the historic forms of celebrating them. The basis of the selection of material was to search out customs that have some relation with past experiences, yet are suitable for a modern celebration. Not in any way does it aim to be exhaustive—rather the material has been chosen with the idea that it might create a desire to give festivals and at the same time furnish a working basis for them. We trust some of these gems of the past still retain their charm and become a pleasant memory for any who experience them.

2. NEW YEAR'S DAY

The old year and the new year meet,
And one goes back to God again
And one stays on for joy or pain.

On New Year's Day, one can almost hear the rustle of new leaves being turned over—ones with New Year resolutions, lovely clean pages on the calendar, and a brand-new ledger at the office. Some people even go so far as to shed old garments and start the New Year with fresh ones.

In America, the biggest, gayest party of the year is usually planned for New Year's Eve. The next day is spent resting, calling on friends and, later on, enjoying a family dinner. Since we are suggesting traditional customs only in this book, we have selected a few that might fit into a modern celebration in the home, church or community. They are to be used as an episode rather than a full evening's entertainment.

Ringing the Yule

Blowing trumpets to the four corners of the world is practiced in many European countries. Near the stroke of twelve, four trumpeters mount to a high tower which dominates the town, where they play a hymn like Martin Luther's *A Mighty Fortress Is Our God.* Sometimes the horn blowers arrange a Christmas melody in which each man sounds a single note on his horn at one time.

When the first note stops, the second begins, the third note follows the second, and so on, until the entire tune is played.

In the British Isles, bells are rung muffled until twelve midnight to show grief at the passing of the old year. On the stroke of twelve, the bells are unmuffled so they sound out clearly to announce the arrival of a new year with its happy promises.

On the first day of the New Year in Japan, everyone goes to the temple to worship in the "four directions"—meaning worship of Gods of the whole world.

First Footing

The tradition of "First Footing" is based on the belief that the character of the first person entering the household after midnight affects its welfare. It was always planned that a fair person should enter first—a good omen for the coming year. The guests bore gifts of cake, bread and cheese and, in turn, the host had a hot pint prepared. Each member drank "A good health and a happy New Year, and many of them," then would follow handshaking and more good wishes.

New Year's Gifts

On New Year's, it was permitted to "ask" for any gift you desired. This custom was practiced by Queen Elizabeth I of England, who took this opportunity to replenish her wardrobe as well as her jewel box. The first metal pins were made during the reign of Henry VIII and were considered to be an agreeable present for a lady. Thus expenses for luxuries came to be called "pin money"—a familiar expression to us. Gloves were also popular as a gift, and a less expensive item. Also, a pomander (orange stuffed solidly with cloves) was a popular house present where a party was in progress. It was used to float in the wassail bowl to add new and delicious flavors.

In France, early in the morning, tradesfolks send errand boys to patrons with "season's compliments," and a gift characteristic of their trade. A fisherman may send oysters, a baker a brioche, a butcher a chicken, a dairyman eggs, and so on. In return, it is

customary to give wine and money to those who bring the presents.

Plundering the Christmas Tree

This custom is practiced on Twelfth Night in Sweden and other North countries, where the Christmas tree is left standing until Twelfth Night. Since we dismantle our trees earlier, the idea can be adapted to a New Year's celebration as well. In the countries where this custom originated, groups of people meet on the village square and then go from house to house to plunder Christmas trees. In each home, the hostess and children dismantle the tree in advance and place the ornaments on a tray. Simple refreshments, such as cookies and a hot beverage, are placed on a table in each household. Each guest is allowed to help himself to a tree ornament, which is usually edible, such as candy wrapped in shiny foil or a decorated cookie.

When all the homes have been visited, the bare trees are carried to the village square to be burned. As the huge bonfire flares up, all the company sing Christmas carols for the last time that season and then join hands to sing *Auld Lang Syne* as the bells ring at midnight.

New Year's In Belgium

The children, for weeks, save pennies to buy gaily decorated colored paper to write New Year's greetings to their parents. They are hidden until New Year's morning, when the children read their little compositions to their assembled family. They not only wish them health and happiness through the coming year, but promise to mend their naughty ways and behave like angels during the next twelve months!

Visiting Day

In the 1840s and for years thereafter, New Year's Day was the visiting day for the men and receiving day for the ladies. Callers began arriving as early as eleven in the morning, as they had many rounds to make before nightfall. On a stand in the hall was a silver card tray into which a few calling cards were placed from last year's stock so the first caller might not be embarrassed by the fact that he was the first.

The refreshments usually consisted of an immense and elaborately decorated cake, placed on a table in the parlor, and beside

it a great bowl of foamy eggnog. On the sideboard in the dining room were whisky straights and brandy straights for those who could not brook the fifty eggnogs before the end of the day. Scattered about the rooms were little cornets of bonbons, *dragées*, and cornucopias filled with nuts.

Eliza Ripley, in *Social Life in Old New Orleans*, gives a further description of Visiting Day during the nineties and at the turn of the century, when social life was not as informal as it is today.

> It was quite the style for a swain to send his Dulcine a cornet in the early morning. All the men wore silk hats that shone like leather. They flocked in pairs to do their visiting. Men of business fulfilled their social duties by stepping into the dining room and taking a brandy straight with a flourish of the hand and a cordial toast to the New Year. The younger element wandered in all day long, hat in hand with a "Happy New Year"—quaff of eggnog—"No cake, thanks," and away like a flash to another house. So the great day wore on. After house doors were closed, cards were counted and comments made as to who had called and who had failed to put in an appearance.

TWO AMERICAN FESTIVALS

In the United States, we have two famous festivals on New Year's Day that have gained national acclaim, and each year thousands of tourists travel to see them. These spectacular events can also be viewed on television, so, we might say, everybody joins in the fun. They are the Tournament of Roses in Pasadena, California, and the Mummers' Parade in Philadelphia, Pennsylvania.

Tournament of Roses

The first parade took place in Pasadena on January 1, 1886. It was sponsored by the Valley Hunt Club, but the original idea is credited to Charles F. Hunt, founder of the club. On this first occasion, the members decorated their carriages and buggies with real flowers and drove them through the streets on their way to

view various athletic events. From this humble beginning, the parade has mushroomed into a pageant unmatched in the nation and perhaps in the world. The "athletic events" are now one of the greatest football games of the season, in a stadium known as the Rose Bowl.

Today, a beautiful queen leads a procession of fantastic floats covered with flowers—not only roses, but thousands of other flowers in exotic forms and colors. Each year a definite theme is chosen so that all entries from neighboring cities can carry out one central idea. Numerous bands are interspersed between the exquisite floats, so a mood of gaiety and celebration is sustained.

The parade is sponsored by the Tournament of Roses Association, and sweepstakes are offered to cities producing the most beautiful or spectacular floats. It can well be imagined that the cost of some floats runs into thousands of dollars.

Another spectacle of the parade is the sight of hundreds of spirited, prancing horses—their silver trappings glittering in the bright sunlight. Skilled riders put them through their paces to the music of passing bands.

Thus, the Tournament of Roses symbolizes the lush and abundant flora so identified with California.

Mummers' Parade

New Year's Day in Philadelphia, is the occasion for a ten-hour spectacle known as the Mummers' Parade. Although the custom originated in England, it was introduced here when the Swedish immigrants settled on the Delaware River. The men welcomed the New Year by dressing in grotesque outfits and roaming around towns and countrysides in gay bands creating fun for their neighbors and townspeople. In those days as much noise as possible was created by shooting off firearms.

Today, the parade is led by King Momus, dressed in gleaming satin and ornamented with embroidery set off by sparkling sequins and bangles. He is attended by startling mummers or maskers in the guise of wild animals or outlaws such as Robin Hood and his men. Some are in gay costumes with high, plumed headdresses made of pasteboard and covered with flowers, baubles and colored streamers. The entertainers wear dresses of figured material with many highly colored ribbons, pointed breeches, gaudy hose, shoulder knots and sashes—they are the musicians and dancers. Throughout the parade string bands, decorated with colorful plumes, march to the traditional banjo rhythms.

It should be pointed out that no women are allowed in the parade. Men, however, impersonate women in colorful events. It is customary for each group, made up of businessmen and private clubs, to choose their own subject for costumes and floats, so there is no continuity of a theme in the parade as a whole. Some individuals dress as comics to amuse the crowd—these are clowns, young boys dressed as girls or even babies, etc. Everything becomes topsy-turvy, with much shrieking of sirens, blowing of horns, peels of laughter and ringing of bells.

The Mummers' Parade extends over a four-mile route and ends

GOD BLESS THE MASTER.

in front of the Judges' Stand in front of City Hall. The business houses in Philadelphia contribute generously for prizes, which total thousands of dollars. It is estimated a million dollars is spent each year on costumes and floats, but the citizens think it is worth it—the parade adds prosperity and renews pride in their city.

TWELFTH NIGHT

As a feast day, Twelfth Night stands second in importance to Christmas in countries along the Mediterranean Sea. It is some-

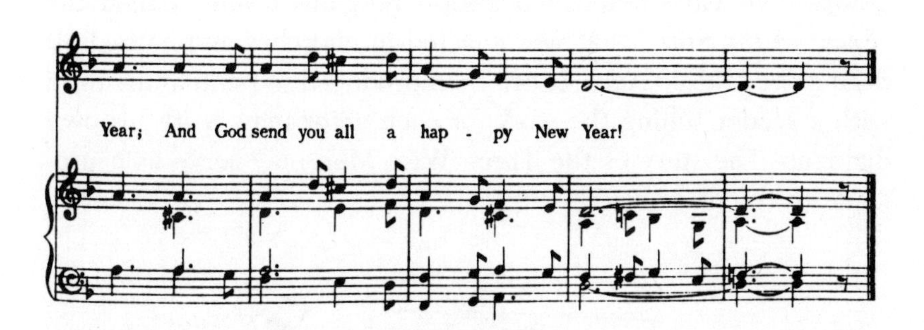

times called "Feast of the Three Kings" because it celebrates the coming of the "Magi" to Bethlehem, where the young Child lay just twelve days after His birth. Each had been told in a vision that they were to meet one another in a certain place in the desert, where they were to follow a bright star onward to the East. They rode untiringly over the sands on white camels until they reached the town of Bethlehem.

The first to arrive was an Ethiopian. He was middle-aged, dark-skinned, and thick-lipped, with a short black beard. His name

was "Balthasar" and he was wearing an Egyptian costume.

The second was a Hindu, an old man with a long beard, and some say he represented *old age*. His name was "Melchior."

The third, a Greek, was young, representing the *future*. He was blue-eyed, beardless, and his name was "Gaspar."

Upon seeing the heavenly infant, they prostrated themselves at His sacred feet with gifts of gold, frankincense, and myrrh. It is said the gold represented the wealth of the East, frankincense was a symbol of purification, and myrrh, an ingredient of oil used for holy ointment, was a perfume.

Twelfth Night in this country is celebrated mostly by religious groups. We have found a beautiful religious drama, called the "*Feast of the Star*," that was enacted in churches and cathedrals during the Middle Ages. It can be reproduced in pantomime form with a reader telling the story, or each actor may write his own dialogue. The story of the Three Wise Men may serve as a prologue to the play.

Feast of the Star

Three priests, clothed as Kings, with their servants carrying offerings, met from different directions in front of the altar. The middle one, who came from the East, pointed with his staff to a star. A dialogue then ensued; and after kissing each other, they begin to sing "Let Us Go and Enquire," after which, the precentor began a responsory, "Let the Magi Come." A procession commenced and, as soon as it began to enter the nave, a crown with a star, resembling a cross, was lighted up and pointed out to the Magi with these words: "Behold the Star in the East." Then all joined in singing the *Star Song*. At the conclusion, two priests, standing at each side of the altar, answered, "We are those whom you seek"; and drawing a curtain, showed them a child, whom, falling down, they worshiped. Then the servants made the offerings of gold, frankincense, and myrrh, which were divided among the priests. The Magi, meanwhile, continued praying until they dropped to sleep; then a boy, clothed as an elf, like an angel, addressed them with 'All things which the prophets said are fulfilled.' The festival concluded with a chanting service.

The following carols, written in the fifteenth century, may be included in the festival. The *Star Song* was written by a country clergyman, Robert Herrick, during the reign of Charles I, and William Byrd wrote the *Lullaby Carol* in 1587. This last carol may be sung when an angel draws the curtain, showing Mary and her Child.

The Star Song

Tell us, thou clear and heavenly tongue,
Where is the Babe that lately sprung?
Lies He the lily-banks among?

Oh, say, if this new birth of ours
Sleeps, laid within some ark of flowers,
Spangled with dew-light? thou canst clear
All doubts, and manifest the where.

Declare to us, bright star, if we shall seek
Him in the morning's blushing cheek,
Or search the beds of spices through,
To find Him out?

Star

No, this ye need not do;
But only come and see Him rest,
A Princely Babe, in his mother's breast.

Chorus

He's seen! He's seen! why then around,
Let's kiss the sweet and holy ground;
And all rejoice that we have found
A King, before conception, crowned.

Come then, come then, and let us bring
Unto our pretty twelfth night King,
Each one his several offerings.

Chorus

And when night comes we'll give Him wassailing;
And that His treble honors may be seen,
We'll choose Him King, and make His mother queen.

Carol, with Lullaby

Lulla, la lulla, lulla lullaby,
My sweet little babe, what meanest thou to cry?
Three kings this King of kings to see, are come
from afar,
To each unknown, with offerings great, by
guiding of a star!
And Shepherds heard the song, which angels
bright did sing,
Giving all glory unto God, for coming of this
King.

Which must be made away, King Herod would
Him kill;
Oh wo, and woful heavy day, when wretches
have their will.

Lulla, la lulla, lulla lullaby,
My sweet little babe, what meanest thou to cry?
Lo, my little babe, be still, lament no more,
From fury shalt thou step aside, help have we
still in store;
We heavenly warning have, some other soil to
seek,
From death must fly the Lord of Life, as lamb
both mild and meek;
Thus must my babe obey the King that would
him kill;
Oh wo, and woful heavy day, when wretches
have their will.

3. MIDWINTER FESTIVALS

Everyone loves a holiday, and during the months of January and February, there are several midwinter celebrations in the spirit of a carnival, with merrymaking, jazz bands, dancing, parades, and much pageantry.

The most important festival in the South is Carnival, which begins with Twelfth Night Revels and ends with Mardi Gras on Shrove Tuesday. In the North, winter carnivals have become the favorite diversion for those seeking a midwinter holiday. They provide not only an outlet for people who enjoy sporting events, but are a great boon for winter-bound inhabitants of little towns and villages in which they are held.

Even though these celebrations are held at the extreme corners of the United States, they have several features in common: each elects a Queen or King, a spectacular parade is always an important feature, music is of a gay tempo, and most of the amenities are informal rather than formal. All of these carnivals are shown on television, but in parts only, so we thought it worthwhile to fill in the historical background and give a description of the most important events.

When the sun rises on Shrove Tuesday, the day before the beginning of Lent, New Orleans—a normal Southern city any other time of year—becomes a community devoted exclusively to revelry, noise, and general madness. For this day is Mardi Gras time, and the Crescent City climaxes the gaiety of its pre-Lenten celebrations and surrenders itself to torchlight parades, fantastic floats, brassy bands, and pageantry unmatched in the nation. All the streets and public buildings are decorated in the official carnival colors, purple, gold and blue, and business is at a standstill.

During the Mardi Gras season, which officially begins with Twelfth Night Revels, some sixty gala balls and countless private parties take place in addition to the parades. The parades themselves are noisy and sometimes ribald spectacles. Fifteen or more floats, elaborately designed with a common theme, comprise the substance of each parade. Added to these are innumerable jazz bands and military marching units filling out every procession until it stretches thirty or forty city blocks. The first parade is held eleven days before Mardi Gras, and nine of the twenty-five take place at night. These are probably more spectacular to watch, not only because they are lighted by flambeaux, but because they draw larger crowds and everyone seems to slip more easily into the carnival spirit after dark.

To a nonresident, Mardi Gras is a blend of four fast-paced days in an old and exotic city. The events are planned by private social organizations called *Krewes,* who produce the parades and finance the balls. Parades are for everybody, but the balls are private affairs, open by invitation only. The Mystic Krewe of Comus, oldest of the city carnival groups, set the pattern in 1857 by staging a lavish parade followed by a ball. This parade and ball pattern is now followed by dozens of organizations which now celebrate Carnival. Among the oldest and most honorable of the Krewes are the Pacifici, Comus, Carnival German, Protens—just to mention a few. Comus still holds the most exclusive ball of all, on the evening of Mardi Gras day, but to Rex, largest of the groups, goes the honor of having Carnival's official royalty—the King and Queen of Rex.

Aside from the parades, there are a number of special events for visitors to see. One is to go down to the harbor to greet Rex as he approaches the Crescent City in regal splendor. Thousands of people gather along the shore to see the royal flotilla with its display of pageantry. Every vessel in the harbor displays, besides the national flags, banners of blue, purple and gold, each bearing the royal crest. Crafts of all descriptions give shrill prolonged sounds of welcome when His Majesty appears on deck, surrounded by his peers. As he steps on land, the royal orchestra strikes a note and everyone joins in singing the royal anthem *If Ever I Cease to Love.* Cheers upon cheers rend the air as the King and his courtiers are carried away to attend a luncheon prepared in their honor.

At high noon comes the fantastic climax to the Carnival. The Rex and Krewe of Comus Parades highlight the day's festivities, and Canal Street is jammed with celebrants and onlookers. All along the route, balconies display the royal colors, and all loyal subjects wear boutonnières of purple, blue and gold. On one of these balconies the carnival Queen sits in regal costume surrounded by her Maids. As Rex rides by in a golden chariot, followed by noisy masked attendants, he lifts his goblet, toasting her to the tune of *If Ever I Cease to Love.*

All afternoon people dressed in costume throng the streets and indulge in all sorts of noisy pranks such as parading, tooting horns, singing and pelting passers-by with confetti and flowers. Many of the maskers toss out gifts as they go along which are merely baubles, beads and bangles, whistles and balls, and the like. Flower-decked cars and floats drive through the streets for hours.

The whole, wild glorious day ends at sundown. Those who like good food go to the French Quarter to eat at one of the famous restaurants such as Court of Two Sisters, Arnoud's and Antoine's. Only the Rex Comus Balls remain to be attended by a list of carefully culled guests, including the King and Queen of Carnival.

If one were fortunate enough to be an honored guest at one of these balls, one would enter a room of unbelievable splendor! Nowhere in the world can be seen more glamorous women clothed in beautiful gowns and sparkling with family jewels. The men are masked and dressed in fantastic, colorful costumes. The ball opens with the orchestra striking a note of the royal anthem, *If Ever I Cease to Love,* in allegro movement, and a Grand March led by former carnival Queens and the present Queen and her Maids begins. Under one of the balconies a space is cleared for the "Call out Section" where black-coated Committeemen roar out names. When a lady's name is called, she is singled out by a gentleman whose identity is concealed by a mask. He proffers a courtly arm, and before they dance, both proceed to pay their respects to the

IF EVER I CEASE TO LOVE.

Written and composed by **GEORGE LEYBOURNE.**

King and Queen. After the dance is ended, the lady returns to her seat bearing with her a favor extracted from the silk sack slung over the masker's shoulder and presented at the moment of parting.

Thus ends the nation's greatest carnival, steeped in tradition and alive with romance. No wonder it attracts dedicated fun-lovers from all over the United States! The church bells ring out early in the morning on Ash Wednesday, and the next day the people in

New Orleans go to church and begin making plans for next year's Carnival.

If Ever I Cease to Love

If Ever I Cease to Love was adopted as the Carnival song because it was so pleasing to an imperial grand duke, and it has been recognized as a sort of royal anthem ever since. It was the Grand

Duke Alexis, who attended Mardi Gras during his Grand American Tour in 1872. Rumor had it that his preference for the song was based on his unconcealed admiration for a certain Miss Lydia Thompson, rather than on any special sentiment for New Orleans' supreme celebration. It was also whispered that it was because the lovely Lydia's rendition of the ditty from the burlesque *Bluebeard* had so entranced the imperial visitor, he singled it out at the time for the Grand March in the Rex parade.

Pancake Day

Shrove Tuesday is called "Pancake Day" in England. People compete to see who can bake the largest pancake, throw it up into the air and catch it on its way down on the griddle in the same flipping motion for which we call them "flapjacks" in this country.

WINTER CARNIVALS

In the North in winter, the annual county fairs and community picnics of the warmer months are replaced by winter carnivals. When snow comes, there is an urge for companionship, a desire to gather together with friends for a social time, so people board trains that carry them to one of the many villages where spectacular sporting events are taking place. The group is made up not only of athletes who go to participate in the different sports, but also of others who delight in watching the winter spectacle and enjoy the amenities of a carnival.

Credit for the first winter carnival is varied. Since 1886, St. Paul's School in Concord, New Hampshire, has set aside a holiday each year for winter sports events. Dartmouth College has established a winter institution with its carnival which was established in 1911. Tourists from all over New England come there to see spectacular feats performed on ice and snow and the magnificent snow sculpture executed by the students and townspeople.

More and more winter sports are gaining the favor of athletes, and we now have many experts. Popular interest in the major sports has created a demand for public exhibitions, contests and competitions, which furnish the real object for a winter carnival. Consequently, new winter playgrounds are being constructed each year from coast to coast. Some are financed by the United States Government, while others are sponsored by nearby cities, athletic clubs, or private enterprises.

No two winter carnivals are alike; some excel in one thing, and some in another, depending on available talents and natural advantages. Each one usually features the outstanding sport of the immediate locality. The main objective is to afford a meeting place for athletes to compete with the best in their field and, at the same time, offer an opportunity for winter vacationers to witness these sports in their best form.

The success of a winter carnival depends on a number of things:

1. The size of the town and the facilities it has to offer for transportation, lodging and amenities for the guests.

2. Natural topography of the country. There should be a ski-jump, toboggan slide, a wide-open field for lesser sports, and also a river or pond for ice hockey and skating.

3. The community spirit and co-operation of the whole town in which the carnival is to be held. Business houses contribute largely in the form of prize money and trophies, and it is often necessary to find lodgings in private homes. All prices should be kept moderate—the town will make money anyway.

In general, a winter carnival lasts three or four days. The whole town turns out the first night for a magnificent parade and to welcome the tourists who have come to witness the spectacular feats that will be performed on snow and ice the next few days. This torchlike parade has become the Mardi Gras of the North with one exception—it is led by the carnival Queen instead of a king. The Queen is usually escorted in a horse-drawn sleigh, followed by the visiting athletes and dignitaries of the town. To make the carnival more festive, some towns select a theme that can be translated to ice and snow, such as Jack Frost Fair, Snow Man Party, Winter Fiesta, etc. This provides opportunities for costumes and settings used in the ice reviews, parades and floats.

It is always pleasant to find a warm welcome. One carnival staged a novel get-acquainted game on the first evening which they called "A Gold Piece Hunt." At the beginning of the evening, five five-dollar gold pieces were placed in the hands of five persons who would mingle with the crowd on the street between the hours of five-thirty and seven-thirty. Each one was instructed to give his gold piece to any person who shook hands and definitely asked for it, provided, of course, he wore a carnival ticket. Any holder of such a ticket could keep the five dollars by simply signing a receipt.

The most interesting thing about a winter carnival, of course, is the program. It should furnish something of interest for everyone, whatever his tastes may be, and enough special events to keep the grounds a scene of excitement from beginning to end. Ski jumping is always the most spectacular of winter sports and when combined with cross-country runs and obstacle races, skiing is the sport that usually highlights a winter carnival. However, do not disregard the spectator's interest in other major sports. Tobogganing and dog races are spectacular to watch, and on ice, hockey and curling are exciting, with so much speed and dash. Also, a baseball game on skates can be lots of fun.

Many visitors are not really sports fans—they come to the carnival to be with friends and look to the town for entertainment. Therefore, in making plans, do not forget to combine the sporting events with social amenities. Begin by listing all facilities the town has to offer—theatres, playgrounds, dance halls, open fields, etc., and select events accordingly. Here are a few suggestions:

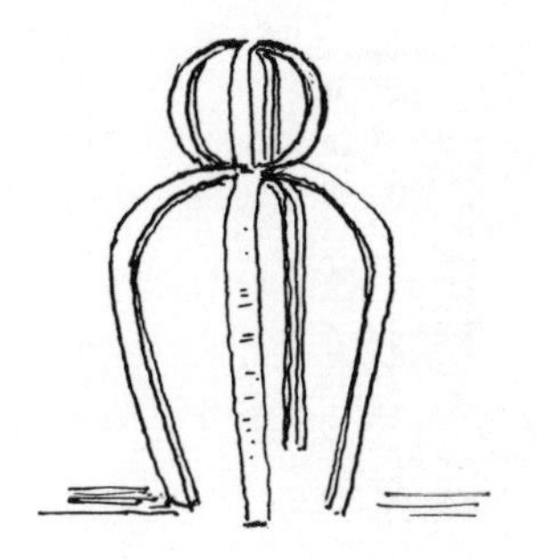

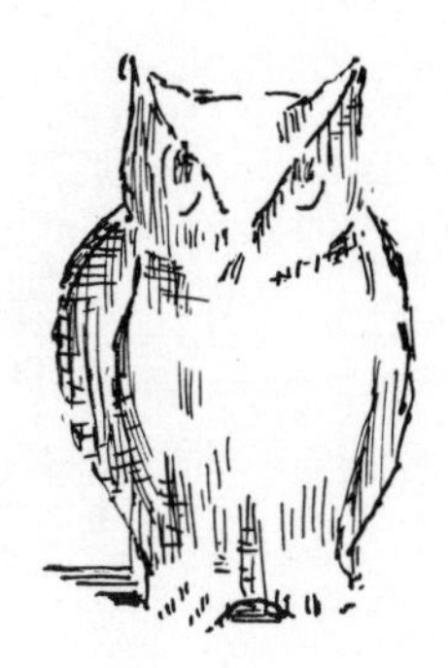

Snow Sculpture

Snow sculpture has become a regular carnival feature, and these forms give expression to various winter themes. The snow man of yesteryear has given way to most elaborate and finely carved figures today, many of which are done in beautiful, sparkling colors.

Sculpturing in ice is really quite simple once you know how to go about it. It can be executed both in relief and in the round. For large statues, use an armature for a framework such as a sculptor uses for clay (see figure above), otherwise the figures must be limited in size. Next, the snow must be wet and plastic rather than powdery. Most sculptors put snow in a bucket, then wet it with a garden hose until it becomes *slush.* The wet snow is then molded to the armature, allowing time between each operation to freeze it in place. If the statue is sprayed while in the process of construction, it will make the work smoother and more solid. Also, when sprayed on cold nights, it takes on the appearance of being carved out of solid ice.

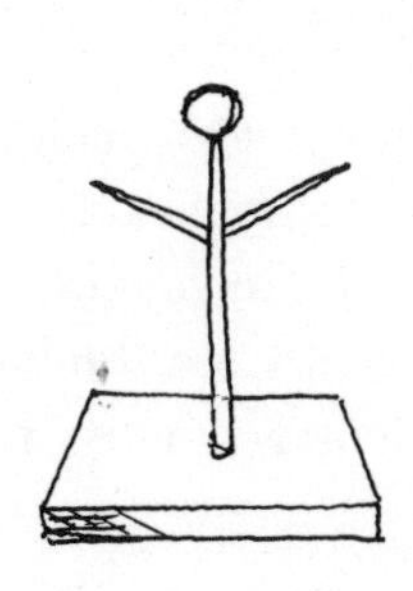

Sometimes the artist prefers to carve objects *in relief* on ice, such as interesting silhouette effects or cameolike heads. To do this, he first makes a wooden mold the size of the cake of ice he wishes for a background. then he fills it with water and allows it to freeze. It is customary in this type of sculpture to color the water so the carving will stand out from a contrasting background. This process is sometimes reversed by using colored slush for the ornament and superimposing it onto a clear block of ice. In either case, the slush is applied directly onto the background and molded before it has a chance to harden. After it becomes frozen, it can be easily chipped, carved and made smooth.

Community Theatre

If you have a community theatre group in your town, carnival time would be an excellent occasion for a production. Plan to give two performances—one for the visitors and the other, either the preceding week or the week after, for the townspeople. If need be, hire some outside talent to please a sophisticated audience—the extra attraction will boost the receipts and make more money in the long run.

Woodmen's Contests

Whenever feasible, woodmen's contests are decidedly entertaining. A favorite one is a chopping competition where green spruce sticks, thirty-five feet to forty feet in height, are set upright in the ground. About twenty-five feet from the base of each, a stake is driven. The logs are to be felled as close to the stake

as possible and then cut in two in the middle. The prizes are awarded to the chopper making the best time and to the contestant who comes nearest to his stake.

Another contest is to cut a quarter of a cord of wood once in two with a bucksaw in the shortest time possible.

A different class in these wood-working contests involves team driving and log hauling. This contest requires two men to harness a pair of horses, hitch them to a logging sled, load on a pile of green spruce logs, and haul them one hundred yards in the shortest possible time.

One other carnival contest in this category is worth mentioning. This one is most spectacular at night, when men mount horses holding a lighted taper in their hands. Each tries to extinguish the other's torch while keeping his own ablaze.

Carnival Clown

Another big drawing card at every carnival is the provincial clown. He is rigged up in a regular clown uniform and keeps the crowd roaring with laughter. The person who assumes this character must be an amazing person indeed—he not only must perform his antics and trickery, but also be a daring fellow as well. Some clowns are skilled enough to jump through a ring of fire or through a paper wall at the end of a ski jump that blocks off his view of the landing below. Whatever the event, skating, obstacle races, tobogganing—the clown makes it exciting for the crowd.

Hootenanny

Since the Hootenanny is so popular on television, it needs no explanation. It is a gathering of people who came with their guitars and banjos for the purpose of singing folk songs. If an entrance fee is charged, it is customary to admit any person free who is carrying a musical instrument. Almost every community has its own group of folk singers, so it would be easy to produce a hootenanny made up of groups from neighboring towns and villages. Look for talent among the carnival visitors—you may find a number of professional singers who would enjoy an evening singing with a group.

Fisherees

Fisherees attract many spectators—the only requirement being a well-frozen lake or bay. Prizes are awarded for the largest or smallest fish, the best fishing costume, first hole cut in the ice, last fish caught, etc. At one carnival, a woman claimed to have won most of the prizes—it developed she was the only contestant that caught a fish!

A Grand Finale

The last night of the carnival marks the climax of what has been an enjoyable winter holiday. A spectacular event should be planned for this occasion that the guests will appreciate and remember. The more important carnivals sometimes stage an ice review or a circus on ice, while smaller communities settle for a square dance on ice or a special campfire program. Some carnivals are ended with a pantomime depicting the end of the winter season such as staging a contest between Winter and Spring, or burn-

a snow man just as the guests are leaving.

No matter what its size, a carnival usually ends with flaming torches and a huge bonfire or even fireworks. A blazing spectacle can be created by throwing out burning snowballs—they are made by slipping a piece of crude camphor, about the size of a chestnut, into the top of a snowball and lighting it at the moment of throwing. Even though no climatic ending is planned, schedule enough special events to keep up a spirit of gaiety until the last snow-train pulls out and the guests have said "good-by."

Hurling the Silver Ball

This is an ancient festival still practiced in many British hamlets. We are adding it to our list of festivals because the idea can

be easily adapted to a contest for playgrounds or camps in this country. At ten-thirty in the morning, a silver ball is thrown into the air by the mayor of the town and is kept moving by the participants until it reaches one of two goals set a mile apart.

The citizens in the town are divided into two equal groups, either according to area in which they live, or by professions. For instance, each side may have an equal number of doctors, lawyers, merchants, bakers, plumbers, etc., along with their constituents. Each group usually chooses a title such as "Ups and Downs," Town and Country," or any name that suits their fancy. The ball must not be allowed to touch the ground, and the game becomes rougher and rougher as it is being carried and battered toward one or the other of the goals.

The silver ball symbolizes the sun at a time of year when earth is at its darkest.

Burning the Bush at Brough

Another version of the above festival is Burning the Bush at Brough. A holly tree with torches on it is carried in a procession in the town. It is thrown to the crowd, which is divided into rival factions, each associated with inns, churches, etc., each hand struggling to gain possession of the burning bush.

CHINESE NEW YEAR

Midwinter is also the time of the Chinese New Year. Unlike our New Year, it begins the first day of the first moon, which means anytime between January 21 and February 19. This fourteen-day festival is celebrated in all Chinese cities, and on each day a special theme is carried out. For instance, the first day is "Family Day"—all members of the families and their households gather together and feast on a meatless diet. On another day, everyone wears his best clothes and, if he can afford it, buys all new garments from skin out. On the fifth day, all houses are cleaned from top to bottom and the dust scattered on running water if there is a brook nearby.

In this country, we are more familiar with the dragon that goes

The Feast of Lanterns.

up and down the street demanding alms or being destroyed. He has a large papier-mâché head to which is fastened a long red velvet train ornamented with embroidery and jewel-like sparklers. A dozen or more men form the legs of the dragon by getting under the train, and the two men in front hold the head high with their arms and hands. A man leads the way by beating vigorously on a drum.

On the last day, all China is aglow with tens of thousands of gaily decorated lanterns. This is called "Feast of Lanterns." The lanterns are made in all colors and shapes and, when lighted, people hang them on porches, in yards, and carry them in parades.

4. ST. VALENTINE'S DAY

Tomorrow is St. Valentine's Day,
All in the morning betime,
And I a maid at your window,
To be your Valentine.

So sang Ophelia, Polonius' mad daughter, as she had a fleeting impression that it was the eve of Valentine's Day—a day set aside for lovers. The thought, however, was but momentary, and the brief image of the lover was soon lost in the vacant chambers of her mind. And so it is today; the day of St. Valentine means hardly more to lovers than it did to Ophelia, and the lacy-edged, flower-bedecked messages of devotion are no longer sent as they used to be in the name of the good Saint.

It is true that now, almost everywhere, St. Valentine's Day is, outwardly at least, a much degenerated festival. The "Whole world loves a lover," however, and the day is still set aside for the Patron Saint of Love, although not nearly as ardently as in the past. Beaux still send valentines with colorful printed designs and sentimental verses; candy in red satin boxes; heart-shaped, beautifully packaged perfume; or flowers—only as a "greeting," and not a "proposal."

Children like a valentine box, with a slit in the top, in which to mail their valentines at school. Do you know there is a certain town in Colorado named "Loveland" whose post office does a land-office business around this special holiday? It all began in 1947, when some individual sent them valentines for remailing. The postmaster stamps them with an appropriate red seal "Loveland" and drops them in the mail again.

Why not have children make replicas of old valentines—they can be associated with the history of our nineteenth century, when our customs and art were dominated by the Victorian influence? To get the teachers started—here are a few of the most important types, along with hints on how to make them. We are also including the history of some of the symbols used for decoration, just to entertain the children.

Symbols Found on Valentines

There have been valentines from the beginning of time yet, oddly enough, the man who originally offered himself as a valentine had nothing so romantic in mind. St. Valentine was a young Roman who was martyred for refusing to give up Christianity. He died in A.D. 270 on February 14, the very day that, by coincidence, had been devoted to love lotteries and to fine-feathered friendships. According to legend, he left a farewell note for the jailer's little daughter, who had befriended him in prison, and signed it "from your Valentine."

Many signs and symbols connected with Valentine's Day are ancient indeed. The red heart, like the red rose, which often crops up on valentine cards, has signified love and emotion since early Roman times.

Ribbons, Laces and Frills

Ribbons and frills have been associated with romance since the days of knighthood, when the chap in shiny armor rode into battle with a ribbon or scarf given him by his lady fair. According to the dictionary, the word "lace" comes from a Latin word meaning to "snare" or "noose"—so its appropriate to a valentine.

Cupid

Cupid was one of the gods of mythology, whose name in Latin means "desire." He is usually represented as a chubby, naked, winged boy or youth with a mischievous smile. He possessed a bow with a quiver of arrows by which he transfixed the hearts of youths and maidens. His darts, some of which were poisonous at the tip, could pierce anywhere.

Cherubs are descendants of Cupid. They are lovable little winged creatures, generally without arrows and quiver. They may be mischievous, but not like Cupid, who aims and draws regardless of the consequences.

The Rose

The rose, which speaks of love, is undoubtedly the most popular flower in the world. By rearranging the letters in the word "rose," we get "Eros" the god of Love. This may explain why it has always been called the flower of romance, the choice of lovers in every century.

Cleopatra contributed much to the popularity of the rose. When she received Mark Antony, she spared no expense in entertaining him royally. Roses, eighteen inches deep, were strewn on the floor, the couches were covered with rose petals and the fountains were filled with rose water.

Empress Josephine of France might well be called the fairy godmother of the rose. She stimulated research in experimental hybridizing of roses with money and grants from her own private fortune. Napoleon's valentine with the rose, mask and fan is probably the most famous one in the world.

Hands

A lady's hand was a favorite decoration. It was not particularly a symbol, but denoted "femininity." Its beauty was enhanced by adding a frilly cuff and a jeweled ring on the third finger.

Clasped hands, of course, represent those of Queen Victoria and Prince Albert and were symbolic of the friendship between their two countries, Germany and England.

Turtle Doves and Love Birds

"Oft have I heard both youth and Virgin say
Birds choose their mates, and couples too, this day;
But by their flight I never can divine,
When I shall couple with my Valentine."

HERRICK

Perhaps the above verse explains why birds were used as a decoration on so many old valentines. It was an ancient belief that birds chose their mate for the year on February 14. Some birds, the pigeon and dove, for instance, mate for life, so they may be used as a symbol of "fidelity."

Violets

There is a legend about the imprisoned young Christian named Valentine. During his confinement, often and longingly he thought of his loved ones and wanted to assure them of his well being. Beyond his window, within his reach, grew some violets. He picked some of the leaves and pierced them with the words "Remember your Valentine" and sent them off by a dove. On the following day he sent more messages which simply said "I love you."

Early Homemade Valentines

The history of the valentine in America appears to have begun during the middle of the eighteenth century. Valentines were laboriously wrought and most were void of lacy frills, undoubtedly for lack of materials. Instead, they displayed fine workmanship in pen and ink, cut paper, and hand-painted designs of flowers, hearts, birds, etc., in elaborate colors. The verses were most sentimental, usually composed by the sender. These early valentines are seldom seen today, but we would like to mention a few of the most popular styles:

Puzzik—About 1840, a quaint sort of homemade valentine appeared. It was in the form of a puzzle which the receiver had to solve. She had not only to decipher the message but also to figure how to refold the paper once it was opened. The order of the verses was usually numbered, and the recipient had a merry time twisting the folds this way and that to determine what was said.

Daguerreotype—This type of a valentine was popular about 1840 and on through the Civil War. It featured an old-time tintype in the center of a card surrounded with an ornamented wreath. In the same class was the "Mirror Valentine" which had a small mirror placed in the center to reflect the happy face of the receiver.

Rebus—This came in many different forms, but usually it was a romantic verse written in ink with certain words omitted and illustrated with a picture to indicate the sense. It was meant to be a riddle and was not always easy to decipher.

Watch Papers—These little watch papers were popular in the days when men carried pocket watches, and they were made to fit within the back or front of a watch, which in those days measured from two inches to two and a half inches in diameter.

Types of Old Valentines

The old valentines on page 39 were chosen not for their historic value, but because they could be more easily made by school children. We are adding a few notes about their structure, but the decoration can be according to taste or material at hand:

1—*Medallion.* An early vogue favored a medallion in the center of a valentine—sometimes it was left vacant for a verse, but more often, it contained the main ornamentation. The area was usually oval in shape, but sometimes it was heartshaped, covered with a piece of crimson-colored satin.

2—*Dressed or Paper Doll* valentines were made around 1860. They consisted for the most part of lithographed faces and feet of boys and girls, with the balance of the figures costumed from various sorts of materials.

3—*Mechanical Valentines* were imported from England. They were constructed so that one or more of the features could be moved by pulling a string. Sometimes the eyes were made to move back and forth, or a hidden tongue would suddenly appear out of a mouth.

4—*Window Valentines* were made with the main motif concealed by a cover of something, such as a door or window. The front of a church was a favorite design—then the door was opened and there stood a bride and groom. During the Civil War, tents were sometimes used, and when the flaps were lifted, a soldier was seen seated on a cot.

5—*Cobwebs.* The process of cutting cobwebs is known as "papyrotamia." They were cut from the thinnest paper and were used to cover the main design like a spider web.

6—*Fine Net Background.* Sometimes the center was removed from a valentine and a piece of fine net substituted in its place. A gay motif was added as shown in the illustration. The delicate perforated background enhanced not only the colors but the importance of the design.

Methods of Decorating Old Valentines

Finding ways to decorate a valentine was a challenge indeed to our great-grandmothers. Materials, if any, were imported from Europe and they were supplemented by nature in the form of grasses, seaweed, pressed flowers and even feathers. Sometimes, only the flower blossom was used, and the stem and leaves were added by hand. Later on, *Swags* of highly colored motifs such as

TYPES OF OLD VALENTINES

1—MEDALLION

2—DRESSED OR PAPER DOLL

3—MECHANICAL VALENTINE

4—WINDOW VALENTINE

5—COBWEB

6—FINE NET BACKGROUND

flowers, birds, butterflies, etc., were shipped over from Germany and were popularly used as ornamentation. They came in double sheets, the top being a highly colored decalcomania while the bottom one was filled with sentimental verses. The following techniques were also used to decorate valentines:

Cameo Embossing. This technique originated in England about 1826 and was sometimes called "paper lace." The embossed designs were copies of real lace but there were no perforations.

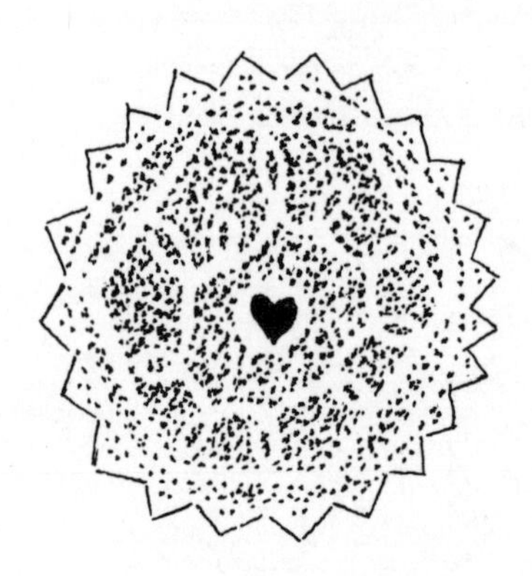

Sometimes the women made them appear more realistic by using a method called *Pin pricks.* This work, as the name indicates, was done by punching tiny holes in the paper with a pin or darning needle. It was used to fill in a definite area or background much as stippling is used on leather or metal. Lace patterns were formed by the same process, only the holes were made with a larger instrument or a knife.

Theorem work was achieved by drawing a design on oil paper. From this a stencil was cut and water colors were used through the cutouts. Gum arabic was then applied to set the color.

Cut Paper Designs—This is a technique familiar to almost everyone. The paper is creased into a number of folds and a design traced on the top fold. The part that is to be cut away is darkened,

and connecting links to all the motifs are left. The background is removed with sharp scissors. The design depends on the number of folds.

Romance Without Words

On Valentine's Day, millions of Americans say "I love you" by sending flowers to loved ones all over the United States. The language of flowers speaks in every tongue, and their meaning is the same today as it was centuries ago. There is a form of "sign language" of flowers that, according to florists, has a tradition of its own:

Just as roses in a bouquet stand for love, leaves in an arrangement represent hope and the promise of fulfillment. A flower slanting to the right means "thou" or "thee," and one sloping to the left "I" or "me." Even specific leaves have come to have their own meaning. A laurel leaf twisted around a bouquet says "I am" and a folded ivy leaf indicates "I have."

The Term "Sub Rosa"

Queen Elizabeth I is said to have worn a rose behind her ear, no doubt copied from the Spanish. Some say this was a subtle way of saying that the wearer "heard all and said nothing."

The origin of "sub rosa" as a synonym for secrecy and silence is

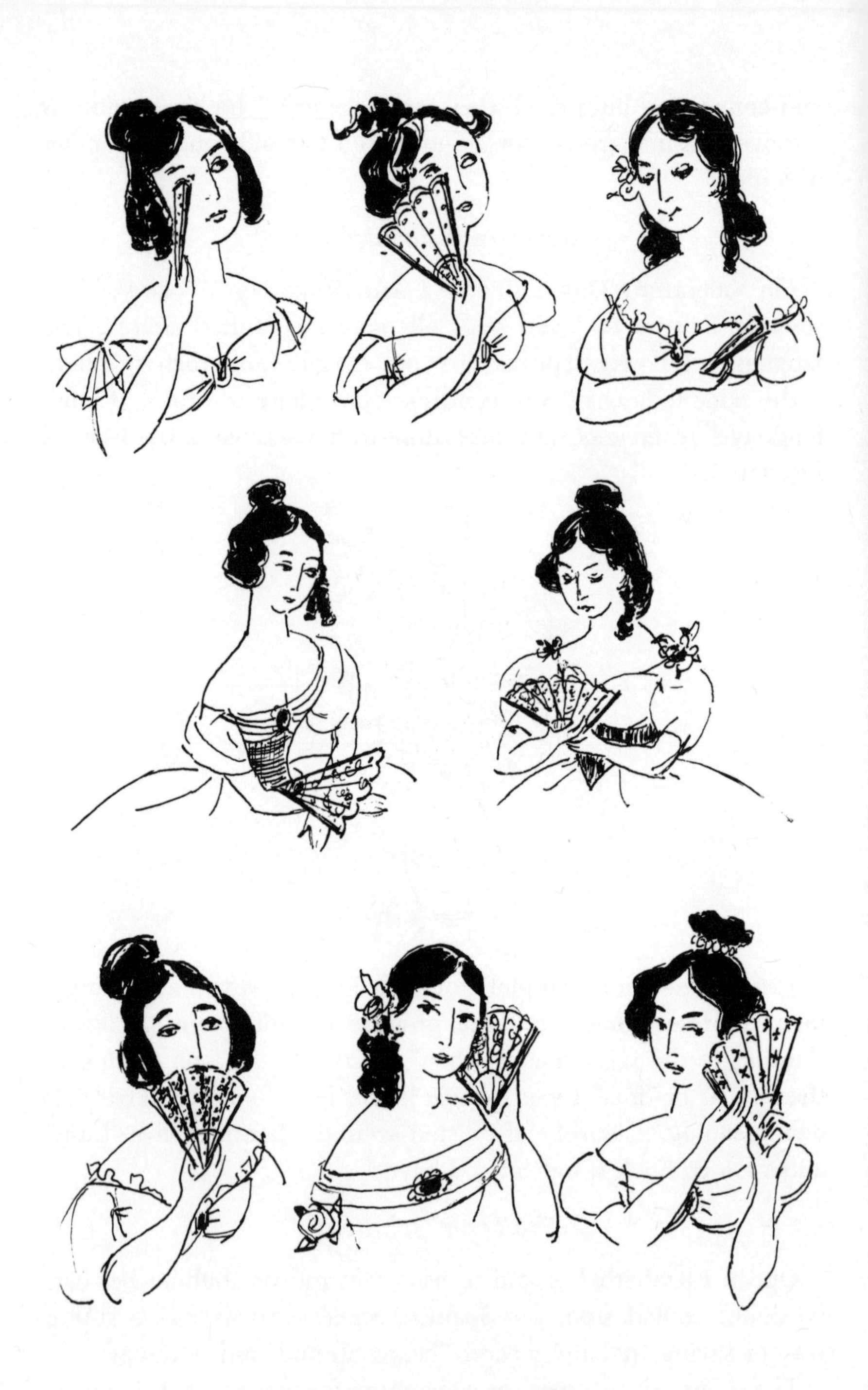

LANGUAGE OF THE FAN

obscure. There are those who claim it was started during the time of the War of the Roses in England. There were two taverns near the Houses of Parliament, one displaying the red rose, the other the white rose. Each tavern was frequented by adherents of one or the other faction, and conferences were held in great secrecy. The participants, in referring to their conversations, would not divulge their secrets, saying they had taken place "under the rose."

Romance of the Fan

The fan is not only a thing of beauty imparting a subtle air of romance and mystery, but it is also an ingenious instrument of communication. In 1879, a code for communication with the fan was registered in the Patent Office in Washington as *The Language of the Fans,* designed to meet the most delicate situation. For example, without her being unmaidenly, the lady's fan in the left hand meant "desirous of acquaintance." However, if she carried the fan in her left hand and gave it a sudden twirl, she would all at once be deserted because that meant "I wish to be rid of you." Resting the fan on the right cheek meant "yes" and, on the left cheek, "no." Dropping the fan coyly suggested "we could be friends," whereas rapid fanning warned "I am engaged."

Language of the Handkerchief

The handkerchief also has its own language, although it is more limited in scope as far as we have been able to ascertain. We do know that the handkerchief thrown over the shoulder means "follow me," and one dropped on the floor for a gentleman to recover says "I would like to meet you." Also, the arrangement of the four corners of a nicely folded handkerchief can signify a message. Perhaps the children would enjoy working out a code of their own.

Bachelor-button

In England, a young man carries a bachelor-button in his pocket on Valentine's Day. If it lives, he marries his current sweetheart; if it dies, he seeks a new one.

5. ST. PATRICK'S DAY

When Irish hearts are happy,
Sure the world is bright and gay,
And when Irish eyes are shining,
Sure they'll steal the heart away.

March 17 is Irelands greatest holiday as well as holy day. The festival is held in honor of St. Patrick, Ireland's beloved saint, and the day commemorates, not the date of his birth, but his death on March 17, A.D. 641. His family were Roman citizens who owned an estate on the west coast of England. As a boy of sixteen, he

was captured by the Gaels (Irish) and was held as a slave for six years, during which time he tended sheep. St. Patrick's life is so strewn with loving legends that separating historical facts from imaginary ones is still a big task for the researcher. Here are some of the wonderful stories the Irish love to tell:

When St. Patrick went on missionary journeys, he was always preceded by a drummer boy who announced his coming. He was captured by the Druids several times, but he made his final escape back to Ireland, where he had fond memories of being a shepherd to the sheep.

St. Patrick used the shamrock to illustrate "Trinity in Unity." He told his followers that the three leaves of the shamrock represent the three members of the Trinity; that the stem was the symbol of the Godhead and of the "Three in One."

The best-loved story, of course, is that St. Patrick drove the snakes out of Ireland. This is only a legend, but the Irish will tell you that you cannot find a snake in all Ireland! One story relates that one old snake refused to leave, so St. Patrick made a box and asked the serpent to enter. The creature objected, saying it was too small. The saint insisted it was big enough to accommodate him and urged him to try it again. After some grumbling, the snake got into the box just to show it was too small, and at once St. Patrick clamped down the lid and tossed the container, snake and all into the sea. The Irish will also tell you that St. Patrick drove the snakes out of Ireland by beating on a drum. Once he struck it too hard and made a hole in it, but an angel appeared and immediately mended it.

The sun refused to set for twelve whole days and nights after St. Patrick died, and stood perfectly still so as not to bring a new day without him. Thousands of mourners came to his funeral from long distances. So many torches and candles were carried that it is said everything was light as day.

St. Patrick's Day also has an agricultural significance. It is on this day that stock are turned out to pasture for the summer. There is an old Irish saying, "St. Patrick turns the warm side of the stone uppermost," and potatoes are planted on that day.

St. Patrick's Day Parade

St. Patrick's Day is not just a great day for the Irish, but for everyone. It has become a good old American custom to wear a bit of green on March 17, even though our ancestors never set foot on Irish soil. All over the United States, the day is one of rejoicing and merrymaking, especially in the larger cities where the streets take on a green haze in honor of Ireland's beloved saint and the traditional St. Patrick's Day Parade. The Irish are known for high spirits and deep feeling, and the parade is a joyful occasion nobody wants to miss.

The St. Patrick's Day parade in New York City is said to have more Irishmen than there are in Ireland itself. Other notable parades take place in Boston, Philadelphia and Atlanta, all cities with a large Irish population. People love watching the parade, not only because it is gay and colorful, but the Irish perform many "hi-jinks" along the way to amuse the crowd. The women wear something green or dress in native costume, and the men carry all sorts of Irish banners along with American flags. The greatest feature of the parade, of course, is the rhythmic music played by dozens of bands interspersed among the marchers. When the bands play such marching songs as *Garry Owen, Top o' Cork Road, McNamara's Band,* etc., everyone joins in the lilt and rejoices with the Irish.

On St. Patrick's Day many thousands of little fabric shamrocks, Ireland's chief emblem, are sold on streets in America. The florist shops also feature little pots of this mystic plant of Irish fame. County Cork is the center of shamrock trade in Ireland, and each year several million plants are sent all over the world. In Florida there is a town named "Shamrock," and fanciful Irishmen like to send letters there to be remailed with the Shamrock postmark.

In Ireland, St. Patrick's Day is on the sedate side; loyal sons of Erin may mark the day by singing of the shamrock and downing another pint for Brian Boru, but they also fill the churches and cathedrals, paying homage to the saint whose blessed day it is.

One feature of the parade that annoys an Irish citizen is the prominence of green everywhere. Ireland's flag is a banner made of three rectangles of equal size—green, white and orange; green representing South Ireland, the Catholic State; orange, North Ireland, the Protestant State; and the white, peace between the two states. In a St. Patrick's Parade, costumes worn by the marchers often include gold and blue colors, in addition to green. The gold represents Ireland's sun and the blue its many lakes. The President's flag is a blue canton with a harp in the center.

Irish Shenanigans

Hostesses planning a St. Patrick's party should keep in mind that the Irish are a carefree, happy-go-lucky race. Serious games should be banned and foolish, hilarious, merrymaking ones be the order of the day. An impromptu program of Irish songs and folk dancing would be most satisfactory to teen-agers, but let's take a look at some traditional Irish games and pastimes that can be played by all ages:

Games involving Irish titles such as Kissing the Blarney Stone, Irish Sweepstakes, Bogs of Ireland, etc., are easy to improvise by adding a few props and applying basic rules of other familiar games. Limericks are fun and not hard to write. Naturally activities from Ireland includes tales peopled with fairies and leprechauns of the Emerald Isle. Many of these folk tales are recorded by famous Irish actors, and the records may be purchased at a music store or found in the local library. Finally, if you would like to include some Irish folk dancing, here are a few good jig tunes: *Blackberry Blossom, Flanner Jacket, Gather up the Money, Tatter the Road, and Irish Washerwoman.*

Paddy's Pig March (Musical game)

Everyone has a partner, but one odd person is given a broom on top of which is tied a paper bag head made to resemble Paddy's Pig. To the strains of Irish music, the guests proceed to march around the room; when the music stops, partners are exchanged. The one who was marching with Paddy's Pig tries to get another partner and the one left without a real partner must march with the improvised Paddy's Pig.

Irish Stew Dance

Music—*Irish Washerwoman*
Numbers—In twos
Starting Position—In rank facing partner, backs of hands on hips
Bars
1– 8 Hop on left foot tapping right toe forward 4 times
Hop on right foot tapping left toe forward 4 times
Hop on left foot tapping right toe forward twice
Hop on right foot tapping left toe forward twice
Hop and tap right, left, right and left toes alternately, forward once.
Bars
9–16 Repeat the toe tapping.
1– 8 Clap own hands together and pass right shoulders with eight skips into place.
9–16 With right foot pointed obliquely forward, drop weight onto it, lift left foot off the ground backward, and incline

Irish Washerwoman

All four gents to the right of the ring .... 2 *Bars*
(Four gentlemen pass to the right.)

And when you get there you balance and swing .... 4 ,,
(Balance and swing the opposite ladies.)

When you get through remember the call .... 2 ,,
(Turn and face corners.)

You allemande left and promenade all .... 8 ,,
(Turn corners with left hands and promenade with lady each one swings.)

Continue this movement, gentlemen moving to right and taking new partners each time.

the trunk forward. Now transfer weight backward onto left foot, bending the right knee upward and hopping twice on the left foot; swinging from the knee (right, left, left, left) or forward, backward, shake, shake). Repeat twice more.

Jump with right foot in front of left and then change with a jump of left, right, and left feet alternately in front.

Bars

1– 8 With left foot pointed obliquely forward, drop weight onto it, transfer weight backward onto right foot, and shake the left leg from the knee twice. Repeat twice more. Jump with left, right, left, right foot changing.

Bars

9–16 Clap hands and pass right shoulders with eight skips into partner's place. Clap hands and eight skips into own place, finishing with a bob curtsy to partner.

IRISH GAMES

Counting Out Game

Riggidy, higgidy, wiggidy, rig,
Paddy dances an Irish Jig,
While feeding potatoes to his pig,
Riggidy, higgidy, wiggidy, rig,
Out goes y-o-u.

Irish Hats

In this game, everyone stands in a circle shoulder to shoulder and hands at side. A hat with bright green bands is placed on the heads of each by a master of ceremonies. On count 1 each man puts his right hand on the hat of the man at his right. Count 2, he removes the hat and places it on his own head. Count 3, he drops his hand to his side. Continue until the master of ceremonies calls "Reverse" and the left hand to hat is used. When the master of ceremonies calls "Stop," everyone remains as he is—any player without a hat steps out.

"Little Pig"

Music: Sing up the scale and down the scale—

I had a little pig,
He had a curly tail;
He became very fat,
So I took him to a sale.
But now that he is gone
I'm feeling quite forlorn.

This is the type of game where the participants are divided into two sides; they sing back and forth—one side using high notes, the other low ones. The words we have given are only to start the game, the players make up their own to finish the saga and keep the game going. A third group singing "Oink, Oink!" may act as a chorus.

Rocky Road to Dublin

Of course, "Rocky Road to Dublin," is a perfect theme for an obstacle race. Obstacles of all kinds—pails of water for Ireland's lakes, things hanging from the ceiling to stoop under and kiss the Blarney Stone, crossing the Bogs of Ireland, etc.

Potato Fortunes

Give each person a potato—the number of eyes in the potato will tell their fortune:

1—foe
2—presents
3—friends
4—suitors
5—travel
6—courtships
7—wealth
8—broken heart
9—happily married
10—single blessedness

The Wearin' O' The Green

DION BOUCICAULT.

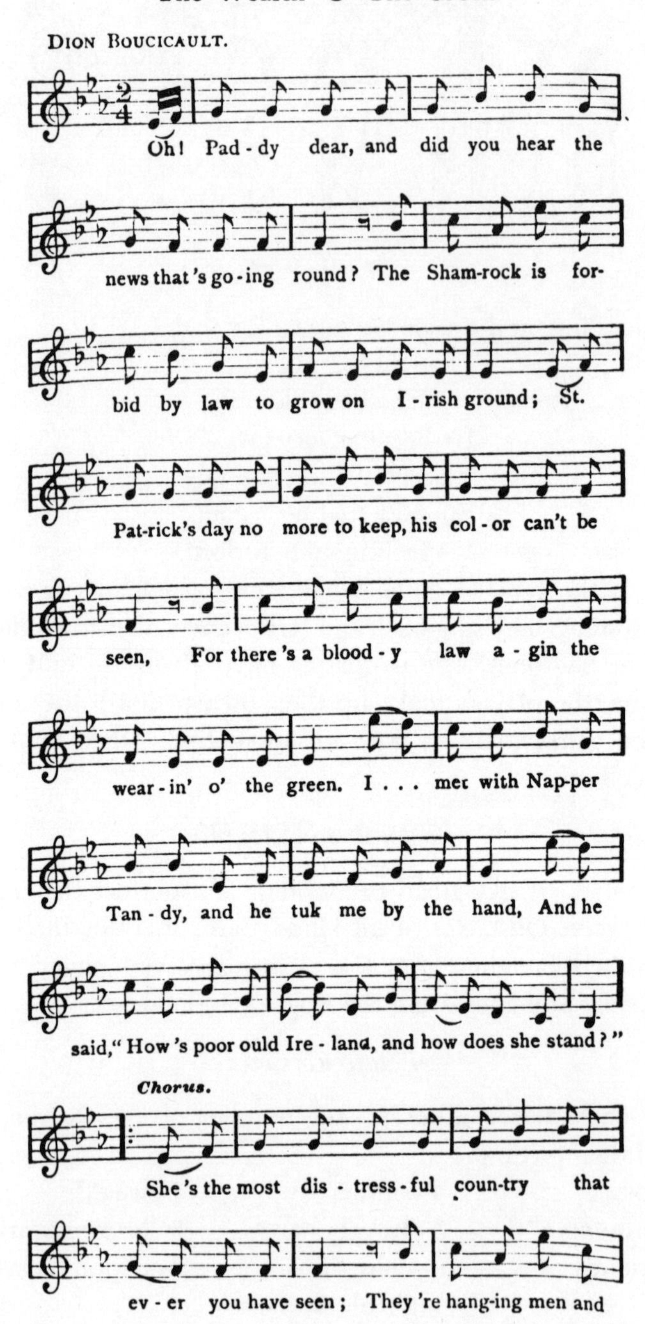

Then since the color we must wear is England's cruel red,
Sure Ireland's sons will ne'er forget the blood that they have shed;
You may take the shamrock from your hat, and cast it on the sod,
But 't will take root and flourish still, though under foot 't is trod.
When the law can stop the blades of grass from growing as they grow,
And when the leaves in summertime their verdure dare not show,

Cho. Then I will change the color I wear in my corbeen;
And till that day, please God, I 'll stick to wearin' o' the green.

But if at last our color should be torn from Ireland's heart,
Her Sons with shame and sorrow from the dear ould soil will part;
I 've heard whispers of a country, that lies far beyant the sae,
Where rich and poor stand equal in the light of freedom's day.
Oh! Erin must we leave you, driven by the tyrant's hand?
Must we ask a mother's welcome from a strange but happier land?

Cho. Where the cruel cross of England's thraldom ne'er shall be seen;
And where, thank God, we 'll live and die still wearin' o' the green.

Irish folk are great tea-drinkers, and this is what the leaves that are left in the bottom of a cup have to say:

1–A ring means marriage. If it is clear, there will be happiness. If the ring is thick and indistinct, someone will try to destroy that happiness by stealing the love of husband or wife.

2–A mountain shows friends of high degree.

3–A clear sun means great good luck. If the sun is thick, on the other hand, only misery is in store.

4–A moon at the bottom of a cup means good luck; in the bottom it shows that, while luck will come, it will take its time.

5–A cross means trouble.

6–A letter with dots all around it means money is on its way. If the letter is in the open and near the heart, a love letter may be expected soon; if entirely in the open, good news is on the way.

7–A tree means health; more than one tree foretells the fulfillment of all one's wishes.

6. EASTER

In Christian lands the greatest religious festival of the year is Easter. It takes place on the first Sunday following the full moon that appears on or after the vernal equinox, about March 21. It is preceded by the six weeks on Ash Wednesday, a period of fasting set aside for mourning the trial and crucifixion of Christ. The season ends on Easter—a joyous day commemorating Christ's resurrection and ascension into heaven. The churches are filled to overflowing with people dressed in new Easter costumes; the altars are banked with lilies and spring flowers; and the choir and congregation join in singing joyous hymns and anthems.

Easter is also a springtime festival, and many customs and legends are pagan in origin and have nothing to do with Christianity. The name Easter comes from the Scandinavian "Ostra" and the Teutonic "Ostern," both Goddesses of mythology signifying the coming of spring. Like all spring festivals of ancient origin, the celebration is closely tied to nature worship; for instance, the symbolic use of eggs and the Easter hare both have a mystical background. Even the ancients knew that all elemental matter is oval-shaped, from the rain drop to the seed, therefore, the Easter egg pays tribute to life's outgrowth of the ancient pagan sacramental cakes eaten by Anglo-Saxons in honor of their goddess, and the Cross is a symbol of many creeds.

Sunrise Services

It was a common belief among the early Christians that on Easter morning the sun danced in honor of the resurrection and people rose long before the sun to see the feat. Sir John Suckling wrote in the *Bride*:

"But oh, she dances such a way,
No sun upon an Easter day
Is half so fine a sight."

Perhaps this ancient belief is the inspiration for the many sunrise services that take place in all parts of the United States on Easter morning. The first such service on record was held by the Moravians in Winston-Salem, North Carolina, in 1773, and it has always been the custom for people in Newport, Rhode Island, to gather along the shore on Narragansett Bay to watch the sun rise up out of the water. The Moravians still hold early services in most of their churches on Easter morning. In Bethlehem, Pennsylvania the rising sun is hailed by the traditional playing of trombones and there follows an hour of joyful Easter music sung by the famous Bach Choir. Two other sunrise services have gained national acclaim and may be enjoyed by anyone turning on the television or radio:

A most elaborate sunrise service is staged in the Hollywood Bowl, Hollywood, California, on Easter morning. It was inaugurated in 1921, and every year an estimated crowd of 30,000 begins to stream in at midnight on Easter eve to spend the night in a dimly lighted stadium. In front of the band shell are 50,000 calla lilies, and shortly after dawn a living cross of 250 teenagers is formed. On the stage is a choir of 100 adults and a symphony orchestra, and as the sun rises over the mountain the service begins. First, trumpet calls are made by six girls clad in flowing gowns, and then a well-known actor reads poetry or a passage from the Bible. The choir, accompanied by the orchestra, sings the beautiful *Hallelujah Chorus* and other Easter anthems.

In Colorado Springs, Colorado, an impressive service takes place in the Garden of the Gods at sunrise on Easter morning. Amid a breath-taking, beautiful setting, people gather to worship in memory of the resurrection of Christ. Music predominates the service and sometimes the three-hundred voice *a cappella* choir of Colorado Spring High School participates.

The Easter Parade

The custom of taking an Easter walk through fields and country still continues in parts of Europe, but in this country, we have a parade. The traditional Easter parade goes back thousands of years when Constantine commanded his council to bedeck themselves in their more elegant robes to observe the day to honor Christ's resurrection. Coupled with this was a popular belief that one must wear for the first time on Easter Sunday a new article of clothing to ensure good fortune for the rest of the year.

In the United States the Easter parade has a different meaning. People enjoy taking off their heavy clothes and donning fresh, light ones of spring and they like to see the Easter parade of gaily dressed worshipers strolling home from church. Outstanding are the ladies' Easter hats trimmed with spring flowers and bright ribbons. Since most of the participants attend church, the parade is scheduled to take place at noon, or at a time when most of the services are over.

The Easter parade in New York City is world-famous. It became an institution along Fifth Avenue late in the nineteenth century and today Radio City and St. Patrick's Cathedral are the focal point of the spring fashion show. People like to view it on television because many celebrities take part in the celebration.

On Mamouth Mountain, near Bishop, California, one of the big annual events has been since 1943 the Eastern Fashion Parade on

skis. All contestants must wear costumes, and the regalia ranges from hobo outfits to the exaggerations of current fashions.

The Easter Rabbit

Why the Easter rabbit hippety-hops into the Easter picture has many mystical explanations. In the Orient, the Easter hare is very closely associated with the new moon, and Japanese artists paint the hare across the moon's disc. The Chinese represent the moon as a rabbit pounding rice in a mortar. The Europeans also have all sorts of fantasies connected with the moon, but the most accepted theory is that it represents fertility. However, we like the old belief that on Easter Sunday a rabbit, after a long winter's sleep, lays bright red and blue, yellow and purple eggs in the new grass.

In Germany, it is the Easter hare that brings the eggs and hides them in the house and garden for children to search for. In many places pretty little rabbit gardens are made ready for the hare. Children have fun making them of moss or grasses to provide a place for the rabbit to hide the eggs. He brings not only dyed eggs of purple, green and yellow, but of wood, and even little pink and blue satin ones. Well known are the eggs made of sugar with little scenes inside that can be seen through a transparent window at one end.

Easter Bells

In France and other Catholic countries, the children are taught that eggs are brought, not by rabbits, but by bells. After Mass on Holy Thursday, the bells fly to Rome to fetch eggs which, on their return, they drop in children's houses and gardens. As no Mass is held and no bells are rung, it is reasonable to think that the bells are away. During this time the bells sleep on the roof of St. Peter's.

Hot Cross Buns

On the first day of Lent pans of hot cross buns are featured in most bakeries throughout the country. Surprisingly, these delicious buns are generally sold only during the six weeks preceding Easter, thus preserving their Christian significance.

The serving of hot cross buns is probably an outgrowth of the ancient pagan sacramental cakes eaten by Anglo-Saxons in honor of their goddess "Eastore." It has been said the early Christian clergy tried to stop the use of these, but instead, the buns were given Christian meaning by being blessed and decorated with a cross. The Italian Tortona, which has its counterpart in many countries, is a twist of dough baked around a colored egg.

One story of the origin of the hot cross bun comes from England.

Hot cross buns date back one hundred fifty years when a widow who lived at Bow in East End, London, was expecting her only son home from sea. On Good Friday she put aside a bun for him, but he never returned. Since that time, patrons of inns have followed this custom in honor of the widowed mother.

Hot Cross Buns!

Hot Cross Singing Game (Another Version)

Numbers—In matched pairs.

Starting position—Stand facing partners, near enough to be able to hold hands.

Hot Cross Buns!	Number 1 cross sits
Hot Cross Buns!	Number 2 cross sits
One a penny,	Clasp right hand with partner
Hot Cross Buns!	Pull each other up to standing
If you have no daughter,	Join right hands with partner
Pray give them to your sons!	Eight skips clockwise
One a penny,	Join left hands with partner
Two a penny,	Eight steps counter clockwise
Hot Cross Buns!	Pull each other up to standing

TRADITIONAL DESIGNS FOR
EASTER EGGS

Easter Eggs

The custom of using eggs in various ways has been associated with Easter for centuries. In Europe, particularly in the Slavic countries, eggs are hand-painted in distinctive traditional designs that are passed down from generation to generation in towns and villages. The making of Easter eggs as presents was at one time almost universal. After they were colored, various designs and inscriptions were etched into the surface and exchanged by those sentimentally inclined, much the same as valentines.

Methods of Decorating Easter Eggs

The stores are full of all sorts of novelties in real or simulated eggs, but it is more fun for people to color and decorate their own. For very small children, it is customary to dip eggs that are already hard-boiled into vari-colored commercial dyes. If you prefer to empty out the contents of the egg before it is decorated, this is the way to do it:

Punch a hole in the small end of the egg and another a little larger by using a push pin or a large needle. A good method of making the larger hole is first to make a circle (a little smaller than a dime) of small holes and then carefully remove the shell and skin inside the circle. Hold the egg, large side down, over a cup and blow through the small hole until all contents are removed.

Etched Design—If the design is to be made up of fine intricate lines, like the ones illustrated on page 8, the usual method is first to dye the egg any background color you wish and then dip it into melted paraffin. After the wax is dry, etch in the design by using a sharp instrument or darning needle. Then dip the egg in a different color dye. Remove the paraffin by heating the egg slightly, then polish the surface by rubbing in the wax.

Designs in Relief. If you wish the design raised somewhat in relief from the surface of the egg, sketch on the motifs with a pencil and then cover the parts to be raised with paraffin. When dry, immerse the egg into very strong vinegar and allow it to remain long enough for the background to be eaten away until the design is raised in relief. Color must be added by hand after the egg is washed and dried.

Cut-Paper Designs. The Polish peasants decorate eggs in elaborate cut-paper designs that is an art form in itself. Usually, the ornamentation is cut out of highly glazed colored paper and pasted onto a white egg, or the process may be reversed by dyeing an egg a color and using white paper for the cutouts. In either case, fold the paper into as many layers as you wish to repeat the motif and make a sketch of it on the top layer. Cut around the outline with a sharp pair of scissors, being sure to cut through all the layers at the same time. Unfold the paper and paste the little cutouts on the egg in a design according to taste.

Easter Egg Games

Eggs play an important roll in Easter sports. Centuries ago, the Romans celebrated the Easter season by running races on an oval track and giving eggs as prizes. Most of our traditional Easter games have the same basic rules as those played by European children, yet there are slight variations in every country. Egg rolling by very small children is a universal custom, yet we find there are many ways of doing that too!

Egg Rolling

Easter comes to very small children on Easter Monday, when it is customary for them to roll their colored eggs down a grassy hillside or slope. The egg rolling on the White House Lawn is famous. Hundreds of children come with baskets filled with gaily decorated eggs and roll them down the famous lawn, hoping the President of the United States is watching the fun. The rules of the game, if followed at all, are to see who can roll an egg the greatest distance or can make the roll without breaking it. Here are some variations older children might enjoy:

A game called "Canigeln" requires great agility and skill. The feat consists of rolling an egg through a ring that has been placed several yards away from a base, according to the age of the contestants.

It is the practice in some countries to use colored wooden eggs for rolling contests. In Central Park, New York City, the children are given wooden spoons to guide the eggs within a lane from twenty to forty yards long.

Egg Gathering Contest

This game is played by older children in England. Eggs are placed at intervals along a race track. Running down the track at a starting signal, the boys try to see who can gather up the most eggs in an allotted time. The game is even more exciting when, as in Germany's Black Forest and some other areas, the contestants ride down the line on horseback or bicycles.

Egg Duels

Spachen is a duel in which the contestants face each other holding hard-boiled eggs by the round ends. Each contestant stabs his adversary's egg with the pointed end. The player who succeeds in cracking the most eggs wins.

Jarking is an old game played at Eastertime. Two boys are given a hard-boiled egg to hold. Then, with their right elbows pressed stiffly against their bodies, and using their wrists only, they attempt to jarr (crack) the top of the egg held by their opponent. The first boy to crack his opponent's egg is acclaimed the victor.

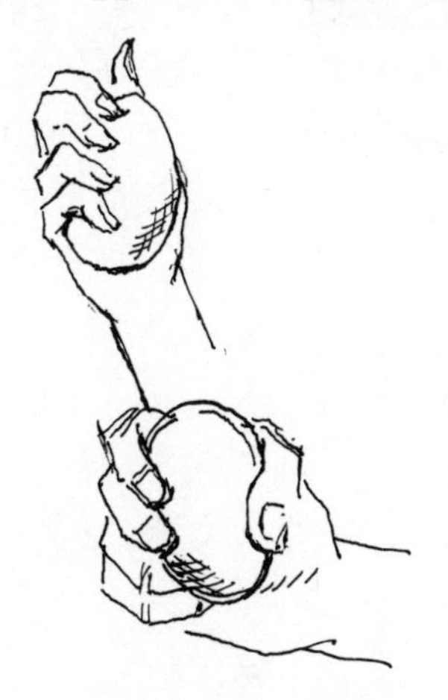

Egg-Wink

We mention this game because it is one of the oldest traditional games associated with Easter. An egg is placed on the ground and

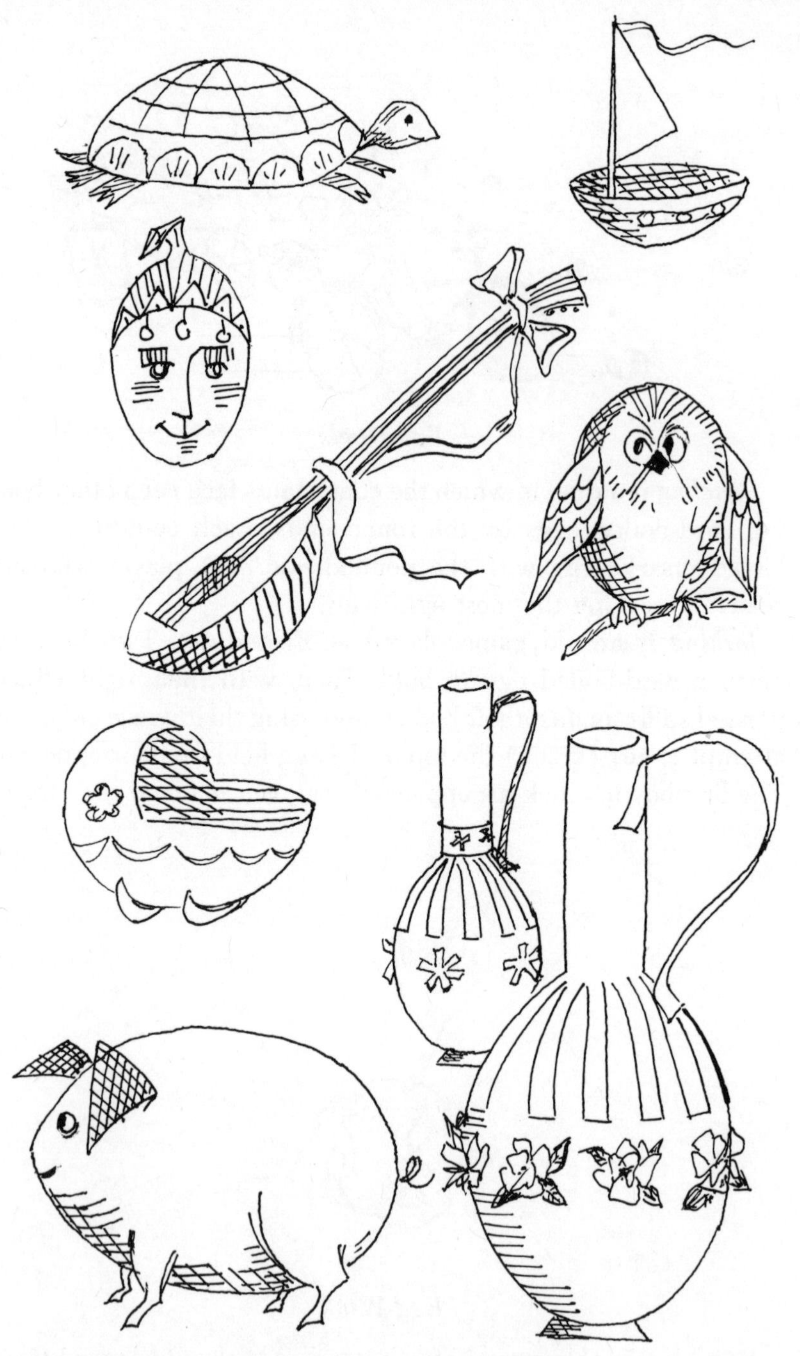

CHILDREN CAN MAKE THESE FAVORS FROM EGG SHELLS TO ADD DECOR TO AN EASTER PARTY

a boy goes back three paces from it, holding a stick in his hand. He then shuts his eyes, takes two paces toward the egg and strikes a blow on the ground with the stick—the object being to break the egg. If he misses, another tries, and so on, until the eggs are smashed.

Easter Bunny's Egg

This is a game small children will enjoy. Make a large sketch of an Easter bunny holding up his paws as if he were carrying an egg and hang it on the wall. Ask each child to make for himself an Easter egg, coloring it in his favorite color, and making it just the size of the space between the Easter bunny's paws. Each egg should have a pin in it. In turn, the children are blindfolded and, from a certain distance, they walk toward the bunny and try to pin the egg in its proper place. The child whose egg is pinned nearest is the winner.

Easter Fashion Dance

This little varsovienne waltz can be used as a feature dance at an Easter party to introduce contenders for the most elaborate

Easter hat, best Easter costume, etc. Each couple, in turn, takes their position on the floor in skater's position and dances the following routine:

PART I

Skater's Position

(Gentleman slightly behind partner, each starting with left foot.)

Three quick, light running steps forward and point toe of right foot to right side	2 *Bars*
Repeat, starting with right foot and pointing toe of left foot to left side	2 "
Repeat above two calls	4 "

PART II

Three Varsovienne Steps to left and point right foot to right side	4 "
Two Varsovienne Steps to right and then lady turns under gentlemans left arm and curtsies while gentleman bows	4 "

(Retard in music here.)

PART III

Waltz	16 "

Egg Dance

The egg dance is very old. To prepare for it, take thirteen eggs, blow the contents from the shell, color eight red, gild four, and leave one white. Place the eggs on the floor in two circles, one within the other. The outer circle formed of red eggs, placed at equal intervals apart, should measure about eight feet in diameter; the inner circle formed of gilded eggs should be four feet in diameter, and the white egg must be placed directly in the middle of the inner circle.

The Dance

The eggs being arranged, the company is divided into couples, each in turn to try the dance. The first couple takes position within the outer circle—that is, between the red eggs and the gilded ones—and, to waltz music, they dance around the circle three times, keeping within the space between the two circles. Entering the inner circle, they waltz three times around the central egg, and all this must be done without breaking or disturbing the eggs.

When an egg is broken or knocked more than twelve inches away from its position, the dancers retire and give place to the next couple. The broken eggs must be replaced and set in position for the new couple.

TWO ORIENTAL SPRING FESTIVALS

Festival of Dolls

On March 3 the Japanese celebrate a gala day called "Peach Festival," for little girls. It has to do with dolls. On this day, all the finest dolls are brought out and placed on exhibition along with rare vases filled with flowers.

The little doll on page 70 is riding to an exhibit in a Kagi. It is a sort of canopied hammock-chair swinging from a pole, the ends of which rest on a coolie's shoulders. Note her fan, parasol, and other accessories rest on the top. The dolls receive guests very formally and tea is served.

Another Doll Festival

In the Indian State of Udaispur, quite a different Festival of Dolls took place every year. This was a country where women were practically shut in their homes and heavily veiled the rest of the year. In celebration of the coming of spring, they were

given one day of freedom, and the women, minus their veils, carry dolls through the streets. The great event of the festival was when the Prince rode by on an elephant to the riverbank where he embarked in his state barge and was rowed around the lake in full view of his subjects.

Festival of Kites

On May 5 is the Kite Festival—a very popular day in Japan. Boys of all ages meet in groups with kites of every description made with Japanese paper and bamboo. The Dragon Kite is always a splendid affair and glitters in the sunlight as if it were covered with jewels.

Large carps made of cloth or paper are an important feature of the festival. They are made with mouths wide open so the wind will come in and puff them up to handsome proportions. They are hung out to fly from poles—one for each boy in the house. The carp symbolizes strength and perseverance because every year it swims upstream and lays its eggs.

The Kite Festival is also celebrated in China; in fact, flying kites is the favorite sport of Chinese boys. Willie Tsang, architect for the Hong Kong Pavilion at the New York World's Fair, recalled "lying in the sun on a rooftop gazing at a sky full of kids' kites, then looking down into the harbor and scanning a sea full of junks." So they provided the theme for the Hong Kong Pavilion. Flying from the ceiling of the restaurant were 500 fireproof Chinese kites through which light from above filtered in every shape and color.

Kite Day at Mill's School

Big kites,
Little kites,
Wee mites,
Flying,
Dying,
Going out to sea,
Was there ever such liberty?
All kinds of sizes,
Out for prizes—
Fighting kites
For boys' rights—
Overhead is Mars,
Among the stars.

MARGARET KIRBY MORGAN

7. JEWISH FESTIVALS

Jewish festivals are joyous occasions, calling for spiritual, religious and cultural expression on the part of those who celebrate. Unfortunately, their beauty and pageantry are not generally familiar to people outside the Jewish faith for two reasons:—first, the celebrations are based on stories in the Old Testament and great events in history pertinent to the Jews in their struggle for freedom in a hostile world; and second, the rituals and ceremonies of most of the festivals are performed within the family circle; therefore, it is necessary to have an understanding of Jewish life in the home.

We have endeavored in this chapter to give a résumé of the important Jewish festivals as they are celebrated in the home. For those not of the Jewish faith, this should be a beginning step toward understanding the religious traditions of a Jewish boy and girl. A trip to a synagogue or temple would further develop knowledge of Jewish religious services and ceremonial objects.

The Arts, of course, speak a universal language when people paint, sing and dance together. It is possible to obtain material for these forms of expression in the Jewish culture from the library,

The Hora

Circle Dance

The Hora is the national dance of Israel. It was originally brought to Israel from the Balkans and has gone through a great many changes, reflecting Israel's development from a barren, neglected land to a modern, throbbing, free country. The Hora is now performed with proud bearing in fast staccato steps and with elevation.

FORMATION: Single circle, arms out to the side, holding neighbor's elbows or shoulders; bodies turned slightly to the left to face counter clockwise. The Hora consists of 6 counts, making the following combination:

Counts 1-2. Take 2 running steps forward in clockwise direction (left foot, right foot).

Counts 3-4. Jump on both feet close together, Then hop on left foot, lifting right foot in place.

Counts 5-6. Facing center of circle, take 3 quick steps in place (right foot, left foot, right foot – the left foot merely tapping).

During the first few measures, the group may face the center and sway left and right several times. The combination of steps described above is repeated over and over again. Towards the end of the melody the group may release hands and clap hands to the rhythm while swaying.

When a teen-age or adult group performs the Hora, they usually continue the steps without a break. It is often accelerated to reach a climax by a series of calls, shouted by one individual and answered by all members of the circle.

HORA - Simplified

Following is a simplified version of the Hora for children and Golden Age Groups:

Counts 1-2. Take 2 running steps clockwise (left foot, right foot),

Counts 3-4. Step-hop on left foot in place,

Counts 5-6. Step-hop on right foot in place.

Simplified "Hava Nagila" Hora

Start with 16 swaying motions, beginning to the left side.

Then do 5 Hora Combinations, 6 counts each.

Then on the "Uru" Chorus, clap hands to the right, then to the left.

Then 4 quick hand-claps forward, each time going higher.

Then clap hands 12 times from side to side.

When the music begins again, do 10 Hora Combinations (6 counts each).

Then on the "Uru" chorus, do the clapping combinations as above.

Records: Folkraft F1431 Zemer Lach
Folkraft F1116 Hava Nagila
Folkraft 1110 Hava Nagila
Israel Music Foundation IMF 119 Sovevuni
Israel Music Foundation IMF LP 6
Folk Dancer 1052
Folkraft 1122
Folkraft 1106

and there are now many recordings of Israeli songs and dances. The Jewish Education Committee Press, 426 West 58th Street, New York 19, New York, also has many helpful publications—notable are three books by Dvora Lapson on folk dances for Jewish festivals, six of which she has kindly given permission to reproduce in this chapter.

Rosh Hashana and Yom Kippur

Rosh Hashana traditionally marks the beginning of the Jewish New Year. It begins the Ten Days of Penitence which culminate in the fasting and in the religious services of Yom Kippur, the Day of Atonement. These High Holy Days are the most solemn of Jewish religious observances. They are a time set aside for earnest self-judgment for individuals rather than a joyous celebration.

This season was designed to soften the erring heart of man with contrition for misdeeds, thus leading him to wholehearted repentance by the time Yom Kippur arrived. The Jewish doctrine is predicated on the belief that "Greater is the merit of the transgressor who repents than that of a saint who never sinned." The reason for this examination and purgation was given by the ancient teachers of Israel: "God gave man his soul that he might keep it pure and in that unsullied condition must man return to Him, for the soul belongs to God."

On Rosh Hashana, services in the synagogues are marked by a great solemnity. After an elaborate liturgy, the *Shofar,* the ram's horn, is sounded. Its clarion call is, as it were, a summons to the worshipers to look within, to search their consciences, and then come to sincere repentance. The belief is that nine days hence, on Yom Kippur, the celestial book of accounts will be closed and judgment reached.

In the Jewish home, the kiddush (the sanctification prayer) is recited, and the festive lights are kindled on the eve of Rosh Hashana. As a piece of sweet apple is dipped in honey, the person who performs this symbolic act repeats, "May it be God's will to grant us a good and sweet year." Likewise, bread is dipped in honey to symbolize hope that, as the bread is sweet, so may the experiences during the approaching year be only the most pleasant. On the second night, some kind of fruit is tasted that has not yet been eaten during the year. Then an appropriate benediction is recited.

Yom Kippur

Yom Kippur is considered the holiest day of the Jewish year, reverently called "the Sabbath of Sabbaths." Many Jews who do not attend the synagogue the rest of the year join their co-religionists in solemn prayer on this holy day. This is the tenth day of the Season of Repentance and lasts from sundown to sundown, in accordance with the Jewish custom for all festivals and fasts.

On the day preceding Yom Kippur, it is the custom for penitents to call on those they might have injured in any way and humbly implore their forgiveness. A large taper is lit in the home as a memorial light to burn during the twenty-four hours of the fast in memory of departed ones.

The Day of Atonement service begins with chanting of the Kol Nidre ("All vows"), the solemn prayer which calls for release from unfilled vows made to God. This dispensation from vows refers only to those which an individual voluntarily assumes for himself alone, and which concern his relationship to his conscience and Heavenly Judge. There is no oath, promise, contract or obligation involving another person, a community, or court of justice in any way.

The "Neilah" is the concluding service of the day, when the worshipers make their final peace with God and their conscience. God's book of deeds is closed and, judgment having been reached, is ready to be opened again for another year.

Purim

Purim, a Jewish semi-festival, is celebrated as a day of rejoicing and thanksgiving, with the exchange of gifts between friends and charity to the poor. It commemorates the joyousness of the Jews when Queen Esther interceded with King Ahasuerus for the deliverance of her people from Haman's vengeance. Indeed, the observance of Purim celebrates the whole story of Esther as told in the Old Testament. "Purim" means "lots," because the day for the extermination of the Persian Jews (the thirteenth day of the month Adar) was determined by casting lots. The thirteenth day

Avinu Malkenu (Prayer)

(Dance for Girls)

Dance by Dvora Lapson

The movements of this dance express the spirit of the song -- a prayer to God to be merciful to us even if we have no deeds to commend us.

Formation: All are dressed in long-sleeved purple robes with sashes around the waist and headdresses of a lighter shade of purple. The soloist stands back center; there is a group on either side of the stage ready to enter in single file. Each group is led by the first person in the line. All have their left hands extended before them and their heads bent low.

PART I.

Phrase 1. The soloist takes 3 slow steps towards the front of the stage, holds one count and continues with 3 more slow steps until she is standing on the forward part of the stage.

Phrase 2. She slowly lifts both hands upward, lifting her head and looking upwards at the same time and ending the phrase by bringing her hands down.

Phrase 3. She takes a step to the right side with her right foot, bending right knee slightly and lifting her right hand up with elbow bent. She ends the phrase by bringing her right hand down and bringing right foot back to place.

Phrase 4. Same as Phrase 3, except that it is done with the left hand and left foot to the left side.

Phrase 5. Facing forward again she lifts both hands upward and accentuates the words "Tzedaka" with an emphatic gesture of her hands and head. On the word V'Hoshienu, she brings her hands down and bends her head low.

PART II. The two lines of girls now enter from the sides and make their way to the opposite sides during the music of Phrases 1 and 2, ending in a semi-circle around the soloist.

The soloist meanwhile sways in place with her hands held out to the side and her head held up.

Phrases 3, 4, and 5 are repeated as in Part I by the soloist and the group.

PART III. All walk off stage with left hands extended and heads bent. The soloist leads and all follow in slow procession.

Our Father, our King! Be gracious unto us and answer us
For we have no good works of our own;
Deal with us in charity and kindness,
And save us.

of Adar is known as the Fast of Esther, and the following day is observed as Purim.

Purim comes in February and, unlike most Jewish festivals, it is secular in nature. The fun of Purim begins with the stamping of children's feet and the noise of the *Greggers* (wooden rattles) whenever Haman's name is used during the reading of the *Megillah* (Book of Esther) in the synagogue on the evening and morning of Purim. Formerly, children's groups would go from house to house in Jewish communities acting out the story of Joseph (in humorous form), singing comic songs and collecting money for charity.

No Jewish festival approaches Purim in its gay carnival spirit. It is marked by all kinds of mummery and burlesque. The mirth overflows from the home into the synagogue, and from the synagogue into the streets and, according to an old Yiddish saying, "Anything can happen on Purim." Children go from house to house singing a popular jingle, the point of which is: "Give me a penny."

Like all festive occasions, Purim, too, calls for special food. During the singing and merrymaking Hamantaschen (Haman's pockets) are served. These are triangular pastries filled with poppy seeds or prunes. *Shalachmones,* gifts of food and drink, are exchanged—the poor being especially remembered.

Pesach (Passover)

The most beloved of all the Jewish festivals is Pesach, or Passover. It celebrates and symbolizes "freedom," a condition cherished among Jews for three thousand years and, for this reason, it is referred to as the "Festival of Liberation." Jewish families, on Pesach night, have always gathered together to relive in recollection their most unforgettable historic experience; their bondage in Egypt and their liberation.

Passover did not always hold this significance for Jews. It had quite a different character in the days when the Temple in Jerusalem stood. At that time, in preparation for the festival, each householder was obliged to slaughter a lamb or a goat—a yearling "without blemish," which he brought as a sacrifice to the Lord. The Festival of Liberation, as we know it today, has been changed because the bringing of a sacrifice into a central place is no longer observed.

I Need a Queen (Dance Pantomime)

Music by S.E. Goldfarb

Dance by Dvora Lapson

Purim is the time for laughter and jest. This dance pokes fun at King Ahasuerus' manner of choosing a Queen.

Formation I: The stage is set with a double throne. On one side sits King Ahasuerus leaning sadly on his hand as he looks straight ahead. He sings the entire song very slowly and haltingly, making gestures as he sings.

PART I

Song	Gestures
I need a Queen, a nice new Queen,	
To sit beside me on the throne;	Points to empty throne.
And if she's very nice indeed,	Gestures to the audience.
I'll give her half the things I own.	Big broad gesture with his hands.
I've looked at maids, so many maids With black, or red, or golden hair	A procession of young girls dressed in long colored gowns come in from right side of stage and walk across as if for a beauty parade, turning in flirtatious manner as they pass in front of him.
But this one shouts,	One girl makes a gesture of screaming, lifting her hands high and in anger.

And this one pouts,	Another stamps her foot and pouts.
And so for none of these I care.	King leaves his throne and runs forward, chasing the girls off-stage left.
	He turns away from the girls in despair. Suddenly he sees Esther, dressed in white, coming on stage right. He makes a gesture of great surprise.
O you are nice, so very nice!	He bows to her with reverence.
Sweet Esther, will you be my bride?	He pleads with her. She hesitates a moment. Then slowly she bows her head in acceptance.
So here's the throne, and half I own, And a hundred and twenty lands beside.	He takes her by the right hand and leads her to the empty throne. She sits down and he takes his own seat. He then places a crown on her head.

PART II

Formation II: Ladies-in-waiting come in from the side in couples with inside hands joined.

Phrase 1. Each one takes 3 steps forward and then nods to the right.

Phrase 2. Each one takes 3 steps forward and then nods to the left.

Phrase 3. Each one takes 7 steps forward and nods forward.

Phrase 4. Partners face each other with dropped hands. Each one takes one side step to the right, then places left foot behind right with arms out and curtsies.

Phrase 5. Still facing each other, each partner takes one side step to the left, then places right foot behind left, with arms out and curtsies.

Phrase 6. Taking each other's right hands, partners take 7 steps around clockwise, returning to own place.

Formation III: Partners in the butterfly position.

Phrase 7. Both take 3 steps forward.

Phrase 8. Both take 3 steps backward.

Phrase 9. Circle around in place to the right in butterfly position.

Phrase 10. Repeat Phrase 7.

Phrase 11. Repeat Phrase 8.

Phrase 12. Repeat Phrase 9, ending by making 2 lines on either end of stage, facing middle aisle.

PART III

Phrases 1- 6. King and Queen dance forward towards audience in the aisle between the 2 lines. Same steps as above Part II, Phrases 1-6. Ladies-in-waiting meanwhile standing in 2 rows on either side sway right and left to the rhythm of the music.

Phrases 7-12. King and Queen and ladies-in- waiting dance same as Part II, Phrases 7, 8, 9, 10, 11, and 12.

End of Dance: The King and Queen then lead the rest of the couples off the stage with the steps of Phrases 1-3.

Suggestion: If there is a program to follow, the King and Queen may, instead of going off stage as indicated above, lead the ladies-in-waiting to the rear of the stage, seat themselves on the throne, with the ladies arranged on either side of them. The King may then clap his hands twice to summon each new number on the program. The group may applaud and show reactions to the remaining performance.

I NEED A QUEEN

I need a queen a nice new queen,
To sit beside me on the throne;
And if she's very nice indeed,
I'll give her half the things I own.

I've looked at maids, so many maids—–
With black, or red, or golden hair —–
But this one shouts, and this one pouts,
And so for none of these I care.

O you are nice, so very nice!
Sweet Esther, will you be my bride?
So here's the throne, and half I own,
And a hundred and twenty lands beside.

Words by S.S. Grossman

As a substitute for the Passover sacrifices and rites in the Temple there was established the institution of the *Seder*.

The Seder

In every Jewish home is a Seder, which means "order." It has a special prayer book called *Haggadah* ("recital" or "story"), consisting, first, of an anthology made up of varied materials of a narrative in epic style, then prayers, benedictions and psalms of praise and thanksgiving. As a sop to the children, it ends with several nursery rhymes and jingles.

Passover begins on the eve of the fourteenth day of *Nissan* (March–April) and lasts eight days, the eighth day having been added during the Middle Ages. But Jews in Israel and those who belong to modern Reform congregations observe only seven days. The first two days and the last two are traditionally considered as full holidays; the intervening ones are only half holidays.

The advent of the festival is marked by elaborate preparations. Special dishes, cooking utensils and silver are used for the entire period. There are special wine bottles, matzoh covers, a *kiddush* goblet, or a benediction cup, for the head of the household. The festival table, too, is arranged in a way reserved for the Seder service and feast.

The night before Passover Eve, in those homes where tradition is closely followed, the ceremony of *bedikat chametz* takes place. The head of the household makes search in all possible places for *Chametz*—leavened bread. This is because throughout the eight days of Passover only *matzoh*, unleavened bread, may be eaten. The custom since ancient times is for the searcher to carry a candle with him and to sweep any bread crumbs he finds into a wooden spoon. At the outset, as a symbol of his search, he places a crumb on a window sill. When he is through, he returns and brushes it ceremoniously into the spoon as he pronounces the benediction "Blessed be Thou . . . who hast commanded us to remove the leaven." The following morning, the leaven he has put aside is burned and the ritual law requires that unleavened bread may not be eaten in midmorning on that day.

The Seder service is conducted at home on the first two evenings of Passover by conservative and orthodox Jews and on the first evening by reform Jews and by the Jews in Israel. The story of the exodus from Egypt and folk songs found in the Haggadah are the focal points of the Seder. In the center of the table is the Seder plate. On it are placed the Passover symbols: a roasted lamb bone and a roasted egg in memory of God's command to Moses on the eve of departure from Egypt and in memory of the festival offerings in the temple; *Maror* (a bitter herb), symbolizing the bitter hardships of slavery; parsley and salt water for the bitter tears shed by the slaves; *Haroset,* made of apples, nuts, wine, sugar and cinnamon, representing the bricks made by the Israelites in Egypt. Cups of wine and *matzoh* complete the symbols used in the Seder.

All members of the family sit in a reclining position at the Seder, commemorating the fact that the Jews were not permitted to sit that way when they were slaves in Egypt. After the benediction, the drinking of the first cup of wine and the eating of parsley, the master of the household breaks the center matzoh. It is customary for him to hide a part of it, the aphikomon (Greek for dessert). Festival folk tradition, which is always gay, requires that the children make a diligent search for it. It is a form of treasure hunt designed to sustain their interest in the long prayer service. At the conclusion of the Seder, whoever has possession of the aphikomon receives a reward.

During the service the youngest child asks his father the "Four Questions" about the why and wherefore of the celebration of Passover. The Haggadah, in a quaint folklore style, describes four kinds of sons who might be asking these questions: the wise son, the wicked son, the fool and the child still unable to phrase the questions properly. To the last one especially the father must patiently and lovingly "explain the matter fully, as it is said. And thou shalt relate to thy son fully on that day." In this manner, not only the memory of the liberation but also an understanding of its significance would be forever preserved among all generations of Jews. Here are the Four Questions:

"Why is this night different from all other nights? On all other nights we may eat either leavened bread or unleavened. Why, on this night, do we eat only unleavened?"

"On all other nights we may eat all kinds of herbs. Why, on this night, do we eat only bitter herbs?"

"On all other nights, we need not dip an herb even once. Why, on this night, must we do so twice?"

"On all other nights, we may sit at table erect or leaning. Why, on this night, do we sit reclining?"

The narrative of the Haggadah is the reply to these questions. The family service finally ends on a note of gaiety. Grownups and children together blend their voices in singing medieval nursery rhymes–*Chad Gadyah* (An Only Kid), *Ehad Mi Yodea* (Who Knows the Meaning of One), *Dayenu* (It Would Have Been Enough) and others. This is because *Pesach* is primarily a festival for children, designed to help them know and cherish the people's traditions of equality and freedom.

Hanukkah

O Hanukkah, O Hanukkah, a festival of joy,
A holiday, a jolly day, for every girl and boy,
Spin the whirling trendles all week long,
Eat the sizzling "latkes," sing the happy songs!
Now light then, tonight then, the flickering candles in a row,
Retell the wondrous story, of God in all his glory,
And dance by the candles' cheering glow.

An Only Kid (Dance Game)

Dance by Dvora Lapson

The traditional Chad Gadyah (An Only Kid), which is sung at the end of the Passover Seder is the subject for this little dance game.

Formation: A group of children arrange themselves in a large circle, one child in the middle representing the kid.

Chorus: Whenever the chorus "Chad Gadyah" is sung, all clasp hands in circle while going around counter-clockwise.

The Cat: When the cat is mentioned, the kid chooses a cat from those in the circle. The cat then enters the circle imitating the movements of a cat and pursues the kid in and out among the others who still have their hands joined in circle until the kid escapes, becoming part of the circle, and the cat takes the center position.

Chorus: The chorus is then repeated as above.

Other Characters: Action similar to the cat and kid episode occurs each time a new character is mentioned, each child trying to imitate the character he is chosen to be and pursuing the character before him in characteristic manner.

If this should be presented on the stage, each child may wear a headdress and a costume to suggest the character he is representing.

AN ONLY KID

An only kid!
An only kid!
My father bought
For two zuzim.
An only kid! An only kid!

Then came the cat
And ate the kid,
My father bought
For two zuzim.
An only kid! An only kid!

Then came the dog
And bit the cat,
That ate the kid,
My father bought
For two zuzim.
An only kid! An only kid!

Then came the stick
And beat the dog,
That bit the cat,
That ate the kid,
My father bought
For two zuzim.
An only kid! An only kid!

Then came the fire
And burned the stick,
That beat the dog,
That bit the cat,
That ate the kid,
My father bought
For two zuzim.
An only kid! An only kid!

Then came the water
And quenched the fire,
That burned the stick,
That beat the dog,
That bit the cat,
That ate the kid,
My father bought
For two zuzim.
An only kid! An only kid!

Then came the ox
And drank the water,
That quenched the fire,
That burned the stick,
That beat the dog,
That bit the cat,
That ate the kid,
My father bought
For two zuzim.
An only kid! An only kid!

Then came the shohet
And slaughtered the ox,
That drank the water,
That quenched the fire,
That burned the stick,
That beat the dog,
That bit the cat,
That ate the kid,
My father bought
For two zuzim.
An only kid! An only kid!

Hanukkah, which means "Feast of Lights," is celebrated in November–December just about the same time as Christmas. The festival begins with the lighting of the first candle of the eight-branched *Menorah*. It is celebrated for eight days with the kindling of an additional candle each successive night until all are burning bright.

Known also as the Days of Dedication, Hanukkah commemorates the Maccabean triumph for religious freedom more than 2,000 years ago. As chronicled in the Book of Maccabees, Judas Maccabeus and his forces triumphed over the Syrian King Antiochus, who had attempted to force paganism upon the Jews.

When the Maccabees recaptured Jerusalem and rededicated the Holy Temple, they found oil seemingly sufficient for only one day. But it burned for eight days. From this are derived the traditions and symbolism of Hanukkah.

The holiday is basically a home festival and one that weaves a special magic for children. There are the gifts (one each night), and the Hanukkah "gelt" (money, mostly gold candy coins, from relatives); the spinning of the "dredil" (a square-sided top inscribed with the Hebrew translation for "A great miracle happened here"), and mother's "latkes" (potato pancakes fried in symbolic oil).

There are the games, the dances and the songs. Young ones gather 'round to chant "Who Can Retell?" describing in verse how "Brave Judas Maccabeus put the enemy to rout, and from the Holy Temple he drove the tyrants out. 'Twas then in old Jerusalem that freedom was attained; and oil of gladness filled the lamp, the Torah lamp regained."

All join hands in the rousing: O Hanukkah, O Hanukkah, a festival of joy, a holiday, a jolly day for every girl and boy. Little wax candles or wells of oil with threads folded together are used as a rule for lights. The lamp is generally placed on the window sill or some other conspicuous place where it can be seen from the outside.

In Israel, there has recently been established a torch ceremony. The torch is lit on the first day of Hanukkah in Modin, the home of the Maccabees, and relayed by runners throughout the country until it finally reaches Mount Herzl near Jerusalem, which is the site of Herzl's tomb.

To Jews in all ages, the story of Hanukkah dramatically demonstrates that there was no force in the world that could succeed in crushing the free and dedicated spirit in man. Rabbi Louis I. Newman of Congregation Rodeph Sholom observed: "The Maccabean spirit of the Hanukkah festival belongs not only to Jewry and Israel, but to all freedom-loving peoples. The preservation of the Jewish faith by the Maccabeans made possible the birth of two daughter religions, Christianity and Islam. The world will always gratefully remember the contributions of Hanukkah."

Old Traditional Dreidel Games

The "dreidel" is a ceremonial toy similar to a spinning top which is twirled by a twist of the fingers. It has a bottom peg on which it spins, a top piece for twirling and four sides, on each of which will be found one of the four Hebrew letters: "Nun" (N), "Gimel" (G), "Heh" (H) or "Shin" (Sh). These are the initial letters of four words which, when put together, make up the sentence, "Nes Gadol Hayah Sham," meaning "a great miracle occurred there."

Because it is not permitted to do any work by the light of the Hanukkah candles, it is customary to indulge in games, riddles and other pastimes to entertain the children during the eight-day festival. The following games are sure to be played:

The old traditional dreidel game was played by the pupils in *Cheder*. The children would seat themselves around the table on which a large Hebrew letter "Peh" was drawn. (The area was approximately equal to a circle two feet in diameter.) Each player started with an equal number of counters from which he contributed to the "pot." The dreidel was spun by each in turn. Each of the letters on the sides of the top indicated a different result of the play. If the dreidel rested with the letter "Gimel" up, it meant the player won the entire "pot." If it fell with the letter "Heh" up, the player received half. If it fell with the letter

"Nun" up, the player received nothing. If it rested with the letter "Shin" up, the player had to add a counter to the "pot."

A second game is one in which the Hebrew letters stand for their numerical values, i.e., "Nun"–50, "gimel"–3, "Heh"–5, "Shin"–300. The players agree beforehand upon a certain goal or limit, and the person who is first to reach the limit previously agreed upon is declared the winner.

Still another game involves skill in spinning the dreidel. A record is kept of the time during which the dreidel is in motion when spun. The player who can spin the dreidel for the longest period of time in a definite number of trials is declared the winner. In addition, it may be required that the dreidel shall remain within a given area (a two-foot circle, for instance) during the time it spins.

The Sabbath

Light and rejoicing to Israel,
Sabbath, the soother of sorrows,
Comfort of downtrodden Israel,
Healing the hearts that were broken.
Banish despair! Here is hope come!

The Sabbath is a day of peace and joy for the Jew, not of solemnity. During the later days of the Temple, the advent and departure of the Sabbath was announced by priests blowing on golden trumpets, and no mourning took place in the home.

The Hebrew poet Bialik introduced the custom of *Oneg Shabbat*, or taking delight in the Sabbath. Groups of people would meet to take part in cultural pastimes appropriate for the day, such as *zemiroth* (religious table songs, folk dancing and singing). These gatherings are very popular in the United States and Canada.

The observance of the Sabbath is ushered in late on Friday afternoon. Not later than eighteen minutes before the sun sets in the western sky, the mistress of the home (generally wife or mother), lights the Sabbath candles and recites a benediction. When the father returns from the special synagogue services after

Have a Little Dreydl (Spinning Top Game)

Music by S.E. Goldfarb

Dance by Dvora Lapson

The Hanukkah Dreydl was originally used for playing with the Hanukkah gelt (money gifts). The dance, a favorite with young and old alike, is a circle game.

Formation: Children arrange themselves in a circle, hands joined and facing the center. One child, placed in the middle, is the Dreydl.

PART I. Children in the circle go around clockwise 16 steps, singing the first part of the song.

The Dreydl in the center, meanwhile, turns in place in the opposite direction.

On the last few counts, the Dreydl choses a partner and pulls him into the center.

PART II. The chorus of the song is now sung.

The children of the circle face the center, and clap hands 16 times as the two children inside the circle whirl each other around, each one getting a chance to be the Dreydl. On the last few counts the child who was originally in the center becomes part of the circle while the child of his choice remains in the middle of the circle, as the new Dreydl.

The music is sung over and over again and each time a new child is given a chance to be the Dreydl.

I HAVE A LITTLE DREYDL

I have a little dreydl,
I made it out of clay;
And when it's dry and ready
Then dreydl I shall play.

O dreydl, dreydl, dreydl,
I made it out of clay;
O dreydl, dreydl, dreydl,
Now dreydl I shall play.

It has a lovely body,
With leg so short and thin;
And when it is all tired,
It drops and then I win.

O dreydl, dreydl, dreydl,
With leg so short and thin;
O dreydl, dreydl, dreydl,
It drops and then I win.

My dreydl is always playful,
It loves to dance and spin.
A happy game of dreydl,
Come play, now let's begin.

O dreydl, dreydl, dreydl,
It loves to dance and spin.
O dreydl, dreydl, dreydl,
Come play, now let's begin.

Words by S.S. Grossman

essing the Sabbath Candles (Ceremonial)

(For Girls)

Dance by Dvora Lapson

On Sabbath eve, just before sundown, the Sabbath candles are lit and blessed by the mother of the family.

Formation: The girl stands in front of the table and faces the lighted candles. Her head is covered with a white cloth.

Phrase 1. While singing this phrase quietly, she places her hands in front of her, waist high, about 10 inches apart, with fingers outstretched and palms turned down.

Phrase 2. The hands are raised upward slowly in a semi-circular movement.

Phrase 3. Same as Phrase 2, but the hand movement is slightly larger.

Phrase 4. The hands are placed close to the face, fingers parted slightly over the eyes. On the word "Sabbath" the eyes are uncovered.

AMEN is sung by all.

"Shabbath Shalom"– all greet each other joyously.

dark, he blesses the children and recites the *kiddush* (sanctification) over a goblet of wine. This is the moment when, no matter how poor, how downtrodden or how rejected a man may be in the world, he achieves dignity and human stature. On the Sabbath, even the most lowly Jew is a king, his wife—a queen, his sons—princes royal.

According to Jewish belief, the Lord blessed and hallowed the Sabbath day (the seventh), the day on which he rested after creating the world. It was to be designated as *Shabbat,* which in Hebrew means "rested." The hallowing of the day was ordered in the Ten Commandments, so that it might serve as part of the Covenant of Israel with the Lord.

There is an allegory in the *Talmud* concerning the Sabbath. The six days of the week stood joined together—only the Sabbath day was left standing solitary and apart. The Sabbath complained: "Why was it so discriminated against?" The Lord explained: "If the Sabbath stood apart from the other days of the week, so did Israel stand isolated in its faith among the peoples of the world." It was meant as a distinction, not a punishment. Moreover, the Sabbath would never be alone, for it was wedded to Israel, who would treasure it forever.

The Sabbath ends after the *Marrib,* or evening service, in the synagogue with the *Habdalah* or "Separation" ceremony, which is repeated later in the home. A candle is lit and then, filling a goblet to overflowing with wine, the worshiper intones a prayer. After reciting the benediction, he opens the spice box which is used in the *Habdalah* ceremony. The smelling of the spices, in which the entire family joins, is a symbolic act, a wishful prayer that the week which lies ahead may be free from care and grief, may be sweet-smelling as the spices and may delight the heart and sustain the spirit.

BLESSING THE SABBATH CANDLES

Blessed art Thou, O Lord our God, King of
the universe, who hast sanctified us by
Thy commandments, and commanded us to kindle
the Sabbath lights.

8. APRIL FOOLS' DAY

APRIL FOOLS' DAY

The first of April, some do say,
Is set apart for All Fools' Day,
But why the people call it so
Nor I, nor they themselves do know.
But on the day are people sent
On purpose for pure merriment.

POOR ROBIN'S ALMANAC, 1760

All Fools' Day has been observed in practically every nation in the world and antiquaries appear unable to trace the custom. The art of fooling people was practiced by the Hindus, in far-away Japan, and in Europe, Catholic churches celebrated the Feast of the Ass. All this seems to indicate that it had a very early origin among mankind, yet none of the dates coincide with April 1.

April fooling is a very notable practice in France, where it is known as "Fish Day." The name stems from the fact that people noted an increase of young fish in the streams on April 1 and that they were more easily "hooked" than the older ones. Perhaps that is the origin of the term "poor fish."

In Scotland, people are sent out on foolish errands such as searching for hen's teeth or pigeon's milk and other foolish items. The favorite joke is to hunt "the gawk" (cuckoo), and anyone fooled on this day is termed an "April gawk."

England also celebrated April Fools' Day and the classical story, "The Wise Men of Gotham," illustrates another type of fooling:

The Wise Men of Gotham

King John, as the story goes, was marching toward Nottingham and intended to pass through Gotham meadow. The village believed that the ground over which a king passed became forever afterward a public road; and not being minded to part with their meadow so cheaply, by some means or other, they prevented the king from passing that way. Incensed at their proceedings, he sent soon after to inquire the reason of their rudeness and uncivility, doubtless intending to punish them by fine or otherwise.

When the men of Gotham heard of the approach of the messenger, they took council, and when the king's servant arrived, he found some of the inhabitants endeavoring to drown an eel in a pond; some dragging their carts and wagons to the top of a barn to shade a wood from the sun's rays; some tumbling cheese down a hill in expectation that they would find their way to Nottingham market, and some employed in hedging a cuckoo, which had perched upon an old bush! In short, they were all employed in such a manner as convinced the king's officer that they were *a village of fools* and consequently unworthy of his majesty's notice.

April First Has Many Moods

There's April Fools' Day, of course,
But there are April flowers too!

Of all the months on the year's calendar, April is perhaps the most invigorating and exciting. It is the time of year when all nature begins to waken from a long winter nap, and the first flowers, crocus, hyacinth, snowdrops, etc., begin to push their heads up out of the ground or even out of the snow. Many of the trees begin to make a show of green, and numbers of birds, whose names and songs are familiar, return from the south to build their nests.

Proverbial wisdom takes, on the whole, a kindly view of this flower-producing month: It asserts that:

> A cold April
> The barn will fill.

The rain is welcomed:

> April showers
> Make May flowers.

And

> An April flood
> Carries away the frog and his brood.

Nor is there any harm in the wind;

> When April blows his horn,
> It's good for both hay and corn.

The Art of Fooling

The successful joker is a merry one—a person who can fool others and create no resentment. The human race has ever been active in inventing new methods to fool each other, and if a person is shrewd enough to please, he is clever. To make a successful April fool, there must be nothing malicious, and a straight lie is unworthy. For example, it is permissible to suggest to a person "that you see several small holes in his coat." The man is horrified and when he says "What! Where!" you quietly say "Buttonholes—April Fool." But to state positively there is a hole in the back of his coat would be a plain lie which does not qualify.

Of course, for successful April fooling, it is necessary to have some considerable degree of coolness and timing, and to know in which direction the victim is most ready to accept the challenge. A large proportion of the business is most effective about breakfast time, before a person has been warned. In some places, tricks are played only in the morning, and if someone tries to play one later on in the day, he is jeered with these words:

"April Fool is past,
And you're the biggest fool at last."

Unfortunately there are cruel tricks, lacking humor and humiliating a person in the eyes of his neighbors, as, for example, telling a man a certain girl wants him to call at her home at a designated time only to find he was not invited and possibly not wanted.

The presentation of mock gifts, beautifully wrapped, can either be fun or annoying, according to the contents of the package. A disastrous one is described in a poem for children written by Charles Lamb:

The First of April

"Tell me what is the reason you hang down your head;
From your blushes I plainly discern,
You have done something wrong. Ere you go to bed,
I desire that the truth I may learn."

"O mamma, I've longed to confess all day
What an ill-natured thing I have done;
I persuaded myself it was only in play,
But such play in the future I'll shun.

"The least of the ladies that live at the school,
Her whose eyes are pretty and blue.
Ah; would you believe it? an April fool
I have made her, and called her so too.

"Yet the words almost choked me; and as I spoke low,
I had hopes that she might not them hear.
I had wrapped up some rubbish in paper, and so,
The instant the school girl drew near,

"I presented it with a fine bow to the child,
And much to her acceptance I press'd;
When she took it, and thanked me, and gratefully smiled,
I never felt half so distressed.

"Ever since I have been thinking how vex'd she will be
Ever since I've done nothing but grieve.
If a thousand young ladies a walking I see,
I will never another deceive."

Perhaps the most successful joke is one where a number of people are fooled at the same time, rather than an individual. There are men who would rather sin than appear ridiculous in the eyes of their neighbors. A classic example of this type of joke was once related by Dorothy Thompson over the radio in comparing "fun tricks" to ones that are often destructive today. Her father was a minister in a small church in upstate New York where most of the congregation arrived in carriages or on horseback. One April Fool Sunday, she and her brother, instead of attending service, busied themselves in the churchyard by changing horses from one surrey or buggy to another. The reward was great watching the farmers sorting out the horses and rehitching them to their own conveyance, but the punishment was also to be remembered, because some of the deacons had no sense of humor!

April Fool in America

April first is dedicated to practical jokers in America. It is not a real holiday; that is, it is not observed by schools, churches, banks or government, but even in our sophisticated society many people, each year, continue to try to fool others whenever they can. In fact, the April Fool idea is still so strong that only a bold man would start an enterprise on the first day of April; and to be married on that day would bring down all sorts of jeers on the courageous couple.

Tricks continue to follow former patterns; alarm clocks will start you off for work an hour earlier, someone will have filled the sugar bowl with salt, the neighborhood children will ring the doorbell and scamper away before the door is opened, etc. Another favorite trick, much too trite to fall for today, is to leave a message to call a certain telephone number and ask for a "Mr. Fox," "Mr. Camel," or a "Mr. Lamb." Of course, the numbers given are ones listed for the zoo or local butcher. In fact, the custom has become so annoying in large cities, the zoo disconnects its telephone on April 1.

April Fools' Day should really be dedicated to little children who delight in telling their elders "there is a hole in your sock" or "a thread on your coat." Boys tie a string to a purse on a sidewalk and conceal themselves with the end of the string in their hand. When someone stoops to pick it up, they pull it out of reach. Then, there is the trick of placing a brick under an old hat on the sidewalk for someone to kick out of the way.

A Typical April Fool Party

Sometimes an April Fool party is more fun for the person who plans it than for the guests who are sure to fall into a trap before the evening is over. Young hostesses, especially teenagers, like to use their creative imagination to give the rooms a topsy-turvy appearance by hanging pictures upside down on the walls, rearranging furniture by setting it in the wrong place (pots and pans in the living room or overstuffed chairs in the kitchen) and, once they get started, the result of their concerted effort is unbelievable!

As for tricks—one can buy a whole bagful at a novelty or ten-cent store. However, a few old ones, if subtly done, can add some merriment to the entertainment. These include gluing a coin somewhere it might have been dropped, thumb-tacking a handkerchief to the floor, covering cotton balls with melted chocolates, etc.

There is no set pattern for an April Fool party—the entertainment is as clever as the hostess who plans it. We can only say, "April days and April showers" put everyone in a party mood and add these proverbs:

> "There's no fool like an old fool."
> "When ignorance is bliss, 'tis folly to be wise."
> "A fool and his money are soon parted."

9. MAY DAY OR SPRING FESTIVAL

May Day is an occasion to make merry, to welcome spring and welcome outdoor play. It is celebrated at a time of year when earth breaks the bonds of winter and clothes itself anew with flowers, and the whole world is glad. May Day, traditionally, is celebrated on May 1, but nowadays, especially in the North, the festival takes place anytime during the first two weeks in the month when the weather is warmer and more flowers are in bloom.

This beautiful springtime festival is observed in every nation—each in its own way. It is believed that May Day celebrations originated with the Romans. They were known to hold an elaborate festival in connection with the arrival of spring. It was called "Florida" and dedicated to Flora, the Roman goddess of flowers. The Greeks also celebrated a spring festival highlighted with athletic games where each victor received a crown of laurel leaves. The custom of celebrating spring was carried to England by the Romans. There, May Day has always been one of the important festivals of the year. In medieval and Tudor England, May Day customs were most interesting and beautiful. Everyone—servant and master alike—was up at the crack of dawn to "go a-Maying." Branches of trees were gathered and brought back to town in a big procession in which the women and children carried wreaths of flowers and the men dragged a long pole to be erected on the village green.

To be chosen Queen was the dream of every girl in the village. Chosen by the lord of the Manor, she might be a squire's daughter or the most modest peasant girl.

The climax of the May celebration was the crowning of the Queen. This was done when the sun was at the highest point in the sky, spreading its warmth and cheer over the greatest area. Merrymaking lasted the whole day, with dancing around the Maypole and sports and games attended by the Queen and her court. Even though May Day festivals are purely local affairs, there are certain highlights or customs that are traditional and included in all May Day celebrations.

The Processional

This part of the festival begins early in the morning, when the whole village goes out into neighboring fields and woods to gather spring flowers. At a designated time and place, everyone gathers to meet the May Queen and escort her, riding in a flower-bedecked chariot, down country lanes to the village.

The procession is led by two small boys in jester's costume with traditionally besmirched faces. Between them, they carry a large hoop fashioned from a long stick onto which are tied spring blossoms, gay ribbon streamers, bells and shiny trinkets. All the children carry sprigs gathered from hedgerows along with little baskets filled with spring flowers. Others carry arched canes with a nosegay and ribbons at the top, and groups of children roll flower-covered hoops.

The processional we have just described is typical of ones usually associated with a May Day festival, yet there are others equally steeped in age-old tradition. For instance in Kent, England, a May Day Festival is held on a grand scale, with a long and spectacular procession of decorated "floats" that approach the city by water. There is much gaiety and festivity along the river-banks as people gather to welcome the Queen.

In other villages, the Queen is preceded by a group of such characters as Robin Hood and his merry men, milkmaids, shepherds and shepherdesses, foresters, Jack-in-the-Green, hobby horses, the King's lion tamer, Morris dancers, jesters, Moll, Mother Goose characters, artisans of all kinds, and villagers with fruits, flowers and boughs. They assemble on either side of the elevation on which the Queen will sit.

The May Queen

"But I must gather knots of flowers,
and buds and garlands gay,
For I'm to be Queen o' the May, mother,
I'm to be Queen o' the May.

TENNYSON: "THE MAY QUEEN"

All May Day celebrations include a central figure in whose honor the event takes place. This gives unity to program. In this festival, it is the May Queen around whom all activities center and to whom subjects pay homage for a day. As the procession ends on the green, a herald (usually a small boy dressed in a red coat and black silk hat) cries, "Silence! Silence!—make way for the Queen who has come to be crowned."

The Queen walks slowly to the dais, her attendants carrying banners decorated with flowers and children scattering rose petals in her path. The actual crowning ceremony is performed by the retiring Queen, who places a crown of fresh spring flowers on her head—she herself wears one of forget-me-nots. The maids of honor dress in white and wear wreaths of flowers with streamers of red, yellow and blue falling from them.

Next the May Tree or Maypole is brought in by a crowd of youngsters skipping happily and blowing whistles made from branches (willow or elder stems). This is called "May music." The tree is set in the center of the green and decorated with streamers, flags, flowers, eggshells and other presents. It is time now to entertain the Queen, and the program begins with dancing around the Maypole.

The Maypole

The Maypole itself is a tall shaft usually painted in gay stripes with colored ribbons hanging from its garlanded summit. The pole should be at least twelve feet high and three inches in diameter. Just below the decorations, about two feet from the top, an even number of streamers, in alternate colors, are securely attached and left loosely hanging around the pole. The streamers should be cut three inches wide and about four yards longer than the height of the pole. Ribbons made of pink and blue chintz are most effective and not as apt to tangle as the paper and cheesecloth ones.

It was the usual custom with old English Maypole dancers to have at least two small boys in the center to hold the pole and help the dancers get their streamers and keep them from becoming tangled. To avoid confusion, only two children should approach the pole at a time to get their streamers.

COMIE, LASSIES AND LADS. May-pole Song

Walking and Tripping Step

This old song may be used for a May-day or May-pole festival as follows :—

Slow walking step with partners for the first twelve bars, and tripping step to the end of the music (eight bars).

The Maypole Dance

Jack-in-the-Green, a chimney sweep, and a group of followers with green boughs head the dancers as they approach the pole. The group collects pennies as Jack proclaims:

"Come all ye lads and lassies,
Join in the festive scene,
Come dance around the Maypole,
That will stand upon the Green."

The children, six to twelve couples, skip in and form a circle around the pole. They skip toward the pole and take a streamer in the inside hand. Girls face right; boys, left. All girls skip to the left of the boys facing them. Then girls skip to the right of the boys coming to face them and boys to the left of the girls. They continue in this fashion of the "Grand Right and Left" until the pole is wound, then skip back and join hands with their partner, skipping around the pole and off the field. Other figures may be added. Music such as *Irish Washerwoman* or *Turkey in the Straw* is played throughout the dance.

Maypole Dance to Waltz Music

Music—Waltz time.

Even number at the pole—every other ribbon of same color.

Partners facing each other.

First Figure: Courtesy to partners (1–4), courtesy to pole (5–8). Repeat. All face left and waltz around the pole once.

Second Figure: Face opposite direction and repeat.

Third Figure: Face left and take glide and hop step once around pole.

Fourth Figure: Face opposite direction and repeat.

Fifth Figure: All of one color streamers step two steps toward the pole and form an inside circle. Others in an outside circle. Inside circle face left, outside circle face right and glide and hop once around the pole.

Sixth Figure: Circles curtsy to each other, face opposite direction and return in the same way.

Seventh Figure: All curtsy to partners and to the pole.

MAY-POLE SONG. Morris Dance and Step

Old Morris Dance Tune, 17th Century.

DIRECTIONS.—The May-pole Song tune, being an old Morris Dance tune, m. be used for the practice of the Morris Dance Step (one, two, three, hop), three wal ing steps and a hop.

The tune, either played, sung, or hummed, may be used for the various May-po exercises and dances.

Two Ancient Customs

Dancing Around the Wells. There was an interesting custom of dancing around the wells, fastening flowers and branches to each one. The cows did not escape. They were decorated with flowers, ribbons, bells and eggs, and were driven through the streets by the milkmaids dancing and singing merrily.

Sanding is another unique feature of the May Festival, a custom said to date back to the days of King Canute who, so the story goes, had forded a stream near Kuntsford just as a wedding procession was approaching. He shook the sand from his shoes in front of the bridal pair, wishing them as many children as there were grains of sand. Whatever the real origin of the custom, the people of Kuntsford are out early on the morning of the festival sprinkling the streets and tracing traditional mottoes and designs in varicolored sand.

Hanging May Baskets

"Hanging May Baskets" teaches children the true meaning of May Day—love, kindness and thoughtfulness toward others. Above all, it is a delightful custom children enjoy.

The hanging of May baskets is reminiscent of the custom of

fastening a bit of green to the porch or doorway to bring a blessing to the house. Today, it means a tribute of love and friendliness, and an announcement of spring and good cheer.

Children enjoy making their own baskets by weaving strips of colored paper, then decorating them with tiny artificial flowers, lace-paper doilies and ribbons. The traditional filler would be:

A piece of candy
A verse
A handful of posies
On top, the name of the person to whom it is sent.

We like the old tradition of a child tiptoeing in the dusk to hang a basket on a friend's front door, then scurrying away before he is caught. Today, it seems to be the custom for the child to be identified.

May baskets are often delivered to mothers, fathers, friends, to sisters and brothers. They also bring cheer to those who cannot attend the May Day celebration—children and friends who are ill, veterans in hospitals, etc. It is a lovely way for a shy child to say "I like you."

Nuts in May

The Game

The children stand in two rows facing each other, about six feet apart. Those in each row join hands. The first stanza of the song is sung by one row, the second by the other, and so on. During the first two lines of each stanza, those in one row walk forward singing; during the second two lines they walk backward.

At the end of the song, the two children who were chosen in the third and fifth stanzas each place one foot against a line on the ground, join right hands, and pull to see who can pull the other across the line. The child who succeeds takes the other child to join his side, and the song is repeated. This time the second row sings first.

Nuts in May

Whom will you have for nuts in May,
Nuts in May, nuts in May?
Whom will you have for nuts in May,
So early in the morning?

3. We will have (Mary) for nuts in May,
Nuts in May, nuts in May.
We will have (Mary) for nuts in May,
So early in the morning.

4. Whom will you have to pull her away,
Pull her away, pull her away?
Whom will you have to pull her away,
So early in the morning?

5. We will have (John) to pull her away,
Pull her away, pull her away.
We will have (John) to pull her away,
So early in the morning.

ENTERTAINMENT FOR SMALL CHILDREN

A Trip to the Woods and Fields

A trip to the woods and fields in the early spring should be the privilege of every child. What joy it is to sit down in the grass and weave a daisy chain, hunt for violets at the edge of the woods, or gather bluebells along a stream. Since wild flowers stem from their roots rather than seeds, children are free to pick them without fear of destroying them, provided, of course, that they do not pull up the whole plant.

During the first warm weeks in the spring, the most delicate wild flowers appear, such as the trillium, anemone, trailing arbutus, spring beauty, etc. Later, sturdier ones like daisies, buttercups, violets and clover can be found in meadows and sunny places. You do not have to go far to look for them—they are in the fields, by the roadsides and even along the edge of streets in small towns and villages.

The Daisy

The daisy means "day eye" because it opens when the sun rises and shuts up and goes to sleep when it sets. It is the most satisfactory flower for children to use for weaving a chain or making a crown because the stem is long and the flower does not wilt as quickly as others. It is a good idea to gather a whole lot of daisies with long stems at the beginning, then put them into a pail of cool water for a while and let them drink a little before working with them. While this is taking place, give each child a daisy and let it tell his fortune:

Daisy Fortune

"Pluck the daisy petals off, saying first 'He loves me,'
With the next: 'He loves me not,'
Then again: 'He loves me,'
With the fourth: 'He loves me not,'
Going on: 'He loves me,'
Till the last, when torn away,
Tells you this: 'He loves you' "

Then continue:

"This year, next year, sometime, never!"

A Chain of Daisies

The simplest method of making a daisy chain is to gather flowers with long stems. Select a daisy and make a loop in the

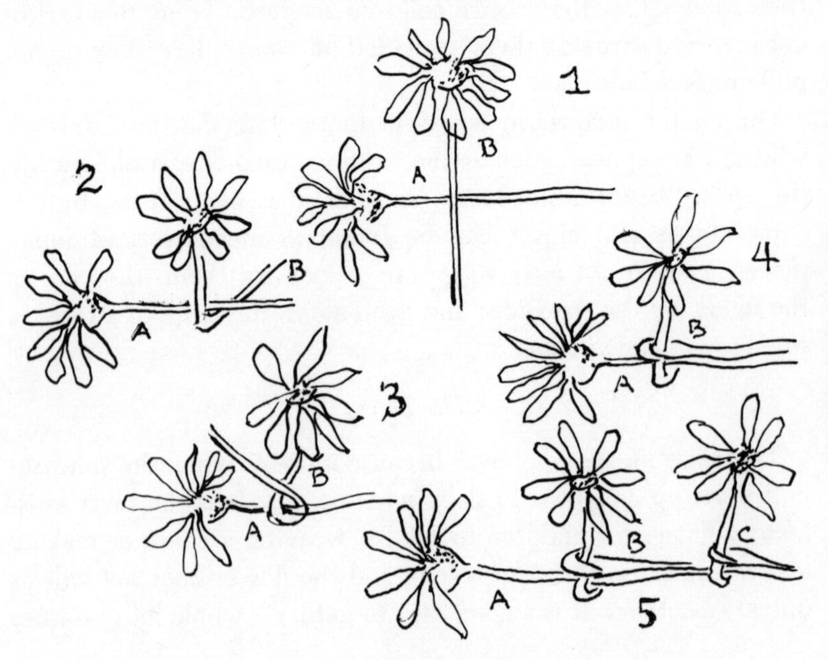

stem just below the blossom. Put the head of another daisy through it, then tighten the loop so as to hold it in place. Another easier method for small children is to push the stem through the daisy's eye and then twist the stems at the back.

A Daisy Crown

Weaving daisies for a crown is a little more complex than into a chain:

1–Cross stem of two daisies, *a* and *b*, just below the flowers as shown in Fig. 1.

2–Now turn stem of *b* under stem of *a* and up at the back as in Fig. 2.

3–Bring the same stem *b* around and in front of its own upright part as in Fig. 3.

4–5 Turn *b* all around the upright; place the stem of another daisy, *c*, below the third blossom and weave it onto the first two stems exactly the same way(Fig. 5).

5–The stems of the fourth daisy will have to cross three stems, *a*, *b* and *c*, the fifth daisy four stems, and so on.

6–The fifth daisy stem will cross the four others, but after that, the daisy stem *a* will probably have been passed and you will be weaving on the others.

It depends on the length of the stems how many are woven over; sometimes there may be five. It is not good to have more than that number. Place the daisies close together so their petals touch or are even crowded a trifle, because the flowers will separate somewhat when curved and brought together. When enough daisies are woven to fit a crown to your head, cut the last stems off about two inches from the last flower, and with a strong blade of grass or a piece of string, tie them to the stem of daisy *a*.

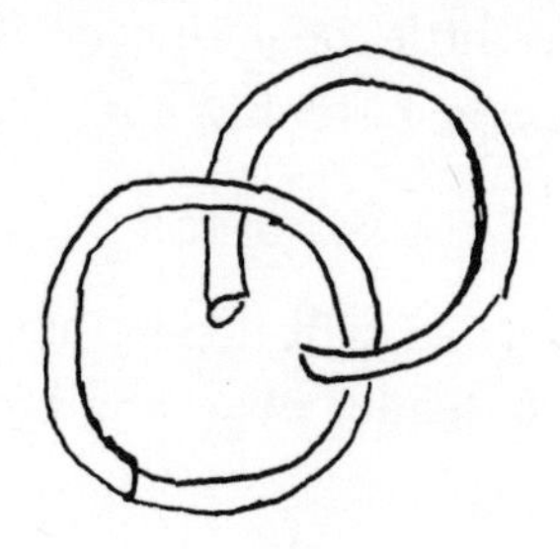

Chain of Dandelion Stems

If you prefer a plain green chain of links, you must gather a great many dandelions and nip off their flowers. You will find that the stem is hollow, and that one end of it is smaller than the other. Push the small end into the larger end of the stem or tube, and you will have a green ring any size you wish to make it. Then put another stem through the ring and join it by pushing the narrow end into the wide one again as in the sketch. If you want the links all the same size, it is best to cut the length at the very beginning.

Chain of Leaves

A chain of ivy or beach leaves makes a pretty ornament to wear while hiking through the woods. This is the way to make one: gather the leaves with long stems and put the stem of one leaf through the top of another. Now pass it back underneath through its own leaf, as shown in the sketch.

Rush Wreath with Flowers

Plait rushes together, keeping strands far apart. Then twine flowers in and out the little open spaces. Tie the ends of the wreath together and cover fastening with ferns or greens.

Oak Leaf Hat

Number of leaves needed will depend on the size of leaf and size of hat. Find smooth, tender twigs and break into short pieces.

Begin by pinning two leaves together in two different places as shown in the illustration. Place first twig near stem and other near lobe and arrange leaves so they meet at the top. Shape to the head, being careful not to make the hat too flat.

May Day Garden Party

If you have a garden or back yard, here is a suggestion for a May Day children's party. Erect a miniature Maypole—the height will depend on the age of the children. It can be made stationary by sinking one end in the ground or placing it in a tub and burying the end in stones and sand. Paint it in bright-colored stripes and use the traditional decoration of placing flowers and fruit at the top and add streamers if there is to be dancing.

Activities other than dancing, can take place around the pole. For instance, children can join hands and dance to the accom-

RING DANCE

The children form in a ring with one child in the center. They all walk around and sing,

In summer, in summer,
That is the time to play,
The children are merry,
And they dance all the day;
And who is standing in this ring
Must do as I do now.

The child in the center then sings:

Just laughing, just laughing,
I do that all the time,
Then will I, then will I
Turn around, and around.

All the children turn around with him during the last lines and all repeat the action of the child in the center as they sing again the last four lines.

Another child steps into the center and the dance repeats. They act different things each time.

panіment of music—beginning with slow time, the music grows faster, faster and faster, and the wheel of children spins around the pole until some hand slips from the one clasping it and the wheel parts.

A Maypole makes a charming setting for circle games, so popular with young children. In games such as the ring dance on page 118, where children imitate actions of the one in the center of the ring, place a child on either side of the pole—half the children can follow one leader and the other half another.

CHILDREN'S GAMES

Maypole Ball Game

The Maypole shown below shows how it can be adapted to a novelty game for children old enough to throw a ball. Six hoops are tied onto a larger one which is suspended from the top

of the pole as shown in the illustration. Wrap the hoops in green paper and add leaves, and tiny artificial flowers or greens if you like. Keep the decorations narrow so the center opening will be wide enough for a ball to pass through. Near the top of the pole, attach four other hoops to make the game more difficult. In the center of each hoop, suspend a small bell which will ring when hit by a ball.

Each child, in turn, takes three steps forward and throws the the ball with the purpose of sending it through a hoop to make the bell ring. The awards, which may be different-colored ribbons or gifts, is a matter of choice. The play goes on until the children are tired.

Flower Game

Two children make an arch with their hands as in "London Bridge" under which all the rest pass singing to the tune of the *Muffin Man* the following verse:

"We're looking for a buttercup,
A buttercup, a buttercup,
We're looking for a buttercup,
And find one here!"

At the word "here" in the song, the two players lower their hands and catch the one who is passing by. He is given a choice between two flowers represented by the two children, and then takes the place of the one he happens to choose.

May-Dew (Music on page 113)

For this game the little ones divide into two parties, one called the roses and the other the dew-seekers. The children on one side provide themselves each with a leaf and then advance singing:

"Here we come gathering May-dew, May-dew,
May-dew, May-dew,
Here we come gathering May-dew,
Early in the morning."

The others, who are supposed to be roses covered with dew, reply:

"Our pretty cups are full of dew,
Full of dew, full of dew,
Which we'll gladly give to you,
Early in the morning."

The roses then all bow their heads. The leader of the other party touches one with her leaf, and the two then take hands and try to pull the other over to her side. The loser joins that party and the game begins again singing the same words. The party who draws the greater number over wins.

Butterfly and Flowers

One child is a butterfly and all the rest are flowers. The butterfly flutters around them until at last it comes to rest near a flower and says: "Fair flower, tell me something about yourself; if you do not, I will fly away with you." If the child can comply, the butterfly kisses her—if not, she is carried away and pays a forfeit.

Tiny little sailboats can be made either by using rose petals or leaves for the bottom of the boat. Cut sail and mast all in one piece from tissue paper. Fold mast over twice according to dotted line. Paste inner sides of folds together and they will form a flat piece, extending out on each side of the mast. On the bottom, spread a bit of strong paste or glue and place mast well forward on large rose petal. The portion of petal which grows near the calyx forms the front or brow of the ship. Be sure the mast stands upright, and allow glue to dry before launching (figure 2 page 121).

Children will enjoy making a necklace of rose petals to wear at the party (figure 1 page 121).

Flower Dolls

Children love to make flower dolls and, while it is entertainment for the moment, they will live in their memory forever. Flower dolls can be made by simply inverting a flower and removing some of the petals. However, it is better to give each child a stick to use as a sort of armature. This enables the child to make the doll more realistic by painting on a face at the top and tying on extra petals for a costume. The doll can be made to stand erect by pushing the bottom of the stick into the ground.

10. HARVEST FESTIVALS

Harvest festivals come at a time of year when the last warmth of Indian summer is gone, and bleak winds and gray skies begin to appear. It is the time of year when barns are made snug, the last of the apples and vegetables are stored away in bins and people sit in front of a roaring fire to relax from their long summer's work. In short, it is a rejoicing over earth's gifts.

The custom of holding a festival at harvesttime goes back over two thousand years. The last day of the year on the old pagan calendar, October 31, served the triple purpose of bidding good-by to summer, welcoming winter and remembering the dead. The Irish built tremendous bonfires on hilltops to offer encouragement to the waning sun and to provide a warm welcome for visiting sprites and ghosts that walked about in the night.

People of the British Isles had the quaint custom of tossing objects, such as stones, vegetables and nuts, into a bonfire to frighten away any "spooks" that might be near. These symbolic sacrifices were also fortunetelling props, still widely used at Halloween parties today. If a pebble a man flung into the fire at night was no longer visible the following morning, people clucked sympathetically, believing the man wouldn't survive another year. If the nuts tossed by young lovers exploded in the flames, theirs would be a quarrelsome marriage, etc.

The North wind doth blow.

More fearful of spooks than spouses, folks began hollowing out turnips and pumpkins and placing lighted candles inside to scare evil spirits from the house. Why was the result called a "jack-o'-lantern"? Tradition says that an Irish Jack, too wicked for heaven and expelled from hell for playing tricks on the devil, was condemned to walk the earth with a lantern forever.

It was the Irish, too, who initiated the "trick or treat" system hundreds of years ago. Groups of Irish farmers would go from house to house soliciting food for the village Halloween festivities in the name of no less a personage than Muck Olla (ancient god of Irish clergy). Prosperity was promised to cheerful givers and threats made against tightfisted donors. It was the custom for English children to dress up in each other's clothes (boys donning girls' outfits and vice versa) and, wearing masks, to go begging from door to door for "soul cakes."

Halloween

Surprisingly, Halloween was scarcely observed in the United States until the last half of the nineteenth century. It is thought the large-scale Irish immigration had much to do with the popularizing of the holiday. Rather than threaten vengeance for youthful Halloween pranks, more and more communities and neighborhoods have been forestalling them with organized treasure hunts, block parties and other forms of entertainment. Just the same, any prudent person on Halloween will see that his car is locked in the garage, porch furniture is stored away and there are plenty of treats, in the form of apples, candies and pennies, to hand out when the doorbell rings and children shout "Anything for goblins?"

DADO DECORATIONS FOR HARVEST PARTIES

Halloween Entertainment

To children, Halloween has always meant phosphorescent paint on skeletons, bats dangling from the ceiling, witches crowded over a cauldron mumbling black magic spells and above all, "wails of the banshee" coming out of the darkness! They love to put their hands under a sheet and hold various (horrible) objects such as a cold oyster, a piece of fur, a bunch of feathers, etc., without squirming. Added to this are numerous jack-o'-lanterns with eerie lights and faces and ghost stories too! All this, we wouldn't change —it is the one night a year in which a child experiences the emotions of fear, fantasy and mystery.

Ghost Walk

Teen-agers might like to have a ghost walk on Halloween, weather permitting. Everyone dresses in white and carries small lanterns as he travels preferably to a place where there are tall rocks, or near a shore. Everyone sits around a large fire and tells ghost stories. A little salt is sprinkled on the fire once in a while to make the setting more ghostlike.

Dado Decorations

A dado is an ornamented border around the lower part of a room (see page 126). This type of decoration is most appropriate for parties given in the fall, when fruits and vegetables are the favorite motifs. These paper cutouts lend color and atmosphere to a party without disturbing the permanent décor of a room.

A Barn Dance or Party

If a suitable barn is not available for a party, a town hall or large auditorium will serve the purpose. Establish an atmosphere with lighted lanterns, place some farm tools and chicken coops around the room and hang garlands of fruit and vegetables on the wall for color. The guests should arrive masked, dressed in ginghams and overalls, and special characters, such as a town sheriff or schoolteacher, should act as master of ceremonies for the party.

Farmer and His Girl (A Good Mixer)

Circle Formation

Ladies four steps to center and back .... 4 *Bars*
Gentlemen four steps to center and back .... 4 „
Face partners and balance and swing .... 8 „
Grand right and left .... 8 „
Meet new partners and promenade in a circle .... 16 „

Repeat from beginning. Note: During promenade all who are left without partners step to center of circle, meet new partners, and continue with dance.

Games such as barnyard scrabble, potato peeling contests, apple-eating race, a husband-calling match, or spelling bee can be included beside the dancing. Here are a few other special features you might like to include:

Jig Contests

The music must be regular square dance rhythm like *Irish Washerwoman, Turkey in the Straw,* etc. Start out with an endurance test, then—

Match girl against girl
Match boy against boy
Mixed contests
Elimination contest

Hop the Pumpkins

Clutter the floor with all kinds of pumpkins, spaced just far enough apart to be a good "hop" away from each other. The pumpkins should be graduated in size so it becomes harder and harder to hurdle them as the player advances. Anyone touching a pumpkin is out of the game.

Husking Bee

A husking bee was a favorite New England celebration every fall. Young people of both sexes shucked corn ears and paid forfeits on red ears by kissing any boy or girl of their choice. The old *Farmers' Almanac,* 1805, asserted, "If you make a husking bee, keep an old man between every two boys, else your husking will turn out loosing!"

Husking for red ears of corn was not the only feature of a husking bee. Its primary purpose was to get as much corn shucked during the celebration as possible. *Contests* were set up to see who could husk the largest number of ears in a period of five minutes. The participants gathered around a pile of corn stalks, dropped to their knees and made the shucks fly. As they husked, each threw the ears back of him and volunteer helpers tried to keep them in neat piles. An experienced hand could husk one hundred and twenty ears or sometimes more than twenty-seven ears a minute.

Afterwards, a hearty supper of baked beans, brown bread and pumpkin pie was served. Sweet cider was the usual beverage.

Five Sheaves of Grain

Place five sheaves of grain on the barn floor and give each sheaf a name such as, Hope, Ring, Money, Charcoal and Thread. Next, go to a henhouse and bring in a drowsy hen or rooster and allow it to walk around and choose one of the sheafs. If it chooses "Hope," it means a long journey of fulfillment of a great wish. The "Ring," of course, means marriage. "Money" is wealth. "Charcoal" portends poverty, and "Thread" means a life of toil.

Means of Telling the Future
Wish on a Star

When the Evening Star appears in the sky, repeat:

Star light, star bright,
First star I see tonight,
I wish I may, I wish I might,
Have the wish, I wish tonight.

Later on, as you go to bed, repeat:

I set my shoes in shape of a "T,"
Hoping tonight my true love to see,
The shape of his face, the color of his hair,
And the everyday clothes he generally wears.

Watch for the star and when it comes, look at it through the branches of a tree. You may possibly find the desired sweetheart.

The Luggie Test

Place seven luggies (bowls) in front of a fireplace and in each, respectively, place—a bit of dough, a rubber band, a sharp thorn, clear water, a tiny elephant and a key. One bowl remains empty. The players, in turn, are blindfolded, spun around three times and told to choose their fate. The symbols in the luggies may be interpreted thusly:

Bit of dough—laborious life
Rubber band—a snappy life
Thorn—thorny life
Clear water—unruffled life
Tiny elephant—lucky life
Empty bowl—spinster or bachelorhood

Witch Writing

If you would like to know how your friends feel about you, here is a test:

Write your name out in full and under your name that of a friend. Then cross out the matching letters thus:

Albert Johnson
Richard Barton

Seven letters cancel out, leaving eleven unmatched. Now begin counting these potent words: friendship, love, indifference, hate—repeat until, on count of eleven, you find your friend is indifferent!

Fortune Jingle

To determine the number of new friends you will find the coming year, count the number of buttons on a dress or coat of the first person you meet after Halloween midnight:

One is good fortune.
Two—a light heart.
Three is a carriage.
Four is a cart.
Five—a new dress.
Six—a new hat.
Seven—a pet dog.
Eight—a pet cat.
Nine—a letter.
Ten—a pleasure.
Eleven—a great joy.
Twelve is a treasure.

Golden Nuggets

Fill a tub with sand and inside place as many golden nuggets as there are guests. Each nugget is in the form of a parcel wrapped in gold paper which contains a trinket or candy with a fortune tied around it. Each player, in turn, takes a shovel and digs in the sand until a nugget is found.

The Three Rings

Several days before Halloween, hang three rings made of braided grass on bushes outside the window sill. Make a wish on each wreath as it is hung in place. To insure fulfillment of the wish, do not see the rings again until Halloween night—your wish or wishes will come true if the rings are not disturbed.

The Shoe Test

Each player, in turn, removes his shoes and, while holding them right side up in his hands, repeats the following verse:

The shoes I toss into the air,
Will they love me dark, will they love me fair?
What future is mine? I pray you show
By the turning of sole or pointing of toe!"

Give the shoes an upward toss and let them fall as they may, and the manner in which they reach the floor indicates the future:

When both shoes land upside down and do not touch, the player will be a great traveler and have no settled home.

When the right shoe is upside down, the future mate will be cross and selfish.

When both shoes land right side up and do not touch, the player will go on the stage.

When the left shoe is upside down, the future mate will be unselfish and kind.

When the shoes are crossed, there will be an early marriage.

When the toes of the shoes point in opposite directions, there will be a decided difference between husband and wife.

When the toes of the shoes point in the same direction, husband and wife will be very congenial.

When the soles cross, lying one on top of the other, the player will own a gold mine!

Cup and Marble Test

Cups and marbles have superficial powers on Halloween too.

Set three cups upside down in a row and under one place a crystal or clear glass marble—under the next one a commie (ordinary brown marble) and under the last, a "China" (a white marble crossed with different lines).

Blindfold each player, in turn, and let the boy or girl raise one of the cups. If the marble under the lifted cup is crystal, the husband and wife will be young and life will be easy and full of sunshine. If it is "China," the husband or wife will be middle-aged, life will be hard but famous.

If the commie turns up, the husband or wife will be old, and life will be filled with adventure.

Note—The marbles must be changed under different cups after each player is blindfolded.

Fun with Apples

No Halloween party would be complete without games with apples, such as bobbing for them in a tub of water, trying to bite into one that is suspended on a string in a doorway without touching with the hands, etc. If you want the apple to tell your future, it will be necessary to eat it first and then count the number of seeds hidden in the core. First of all, the old country rhyme will tell you—

One—I love,
Two—I love,
Three—I love, they say,
Four—I love with all my heart,
Five—I cast away.
Six—she loves,
Seven—he loves,
Eight—both love,
Nine—he comes,
Ten—he tarries,
Eleven—he courts,
Twelve—they marry.

Tasting Apple Seeds

In preparing a Halloween party, dip a number of apple seeds into different flavorings and allow them to dry. Spread them out on a piece of waxed paper and suggest the guests, in turn, select one and place it on the tongue to taste it. Here is a key to the different flavors:

Ground cloves—Life companion never dull or uninteresting.
Pepper—Denotes quick temper.
Cinnamon—Lively, buoyant and bright.
Vinegar—Cross and sour.
Molasses—Loving but stupid.
Lemon—Refreshing and interesting.

Add as many more as you like.

Apple and Toothpick Fortune

You can ascertain for your guests the nationality of their future husbands or wives by giving each an apple and a toothpick. Each player must push the toothpick into any part of the apple he wishes—the spot it occupies tells the fortune, but all apples must be standing upright as shown in the illustration.

When the toothpick stands straight and erect in the top of the apple, the life partner will be an American. If in the left side of the apple, the mate will be English. In the right side, French; in the back, German; in the front, Italian; sideways at the top of the apple, the mate will be West Indian; sideways in the right side, the mate will be Japanese; in the left side, a Russian; and in the front, Spanish. When the toothpick breaks, the player will not marry.

Three Other Fortunes

Stick an apple seed on each eyelid and name one "Home" and the other "Travel." Bat both eyelids and if the seed named "Travel" stays on longest, you will go on a journey before the year is over. If "Home" clings longest, you will remain at home.

Again—

Take all the seeds from one apple, place them on the back of your outspread left hand and strike the palm with your right. This will cause some, if not all, of the seeds to fall off. Those left on your hand will show the number of letters you will receive the coming fortnight. If all fall off, you must wait patiently for your mail.

Finally—

> I pare this pippin round and round again,
> My sweetheart's name to flourish on the plain;
> I fling the unbroken paring over my head,
> My sweetheart's letter on the ground to read.

11. THANKSGIVING – A HARVEST FESTIVAL

In harvest time, harvest folke, servants and all,
Should make all together, good cheer in the hall;
And fill one the black bowl, so blithe to the song,
And let them be merry all harvest time long.

TUSSER

Harvest festivals, traditionally, were not only a scene of merriment and hospitality but a time for a temporary suspension of equality between master and servant. In many places, indeed, this manner of freedom existed during the whole period of getting in the harvest. After the harvest is home, it is the most natural thing in the world for people to laugh and sing after their barns are full and their work in the hot summer is over. Hence—a Harvest Festival. It is a wonderful way to express joy and give thanks for something that has happened.

In the United States, Thanksgiving is more of a "feast day" than any other holiday on the calendar. It comes at the time of year when New England country folk used to slaughter animals and salt them down for the year; the cellars were full of apples and late vegetables (pumpkins, turnips, parsnips, carrots, etc.); and turkeys and geese were in their prime. Also, to most people, Thanksgiving dinner marked the last big meal of the season. Everyone knew full well that winter was fast approaching, when food would not be too plentiful and quite lacking in variety.

The First Thanksgiving

It was the autumn of 1621, in Plymouth Colony, when Governor Bradford, following the custom that had been observed in one way or another for many centuries, set a time for giving thanks for the year's harvest, meager as it was. He also decided to make it an occasion for strengthening friendship with the Indians, so an invitation was sent to Chief Massasoit and his braves to share in the festival. The Indians were pleased to accept and sent five deer ahead as a gift for the feast. Governor Bradford then sent out four men to shoot game, and they returned heavily laden, particularly with wild turkey. In the meantime, the women in the Colony ground meal for corn bread, cracked corn for hominy and gathered cranberries, which they had learned how to prepare. Others prepared huge fires, as the first Thanksgiving dinner was cooked and served out-of-doors.

Massasoit and ninety Indians sat down with the Pilgrims to the first Thanksgiving table in America. All the preparation ahead of time was providential because, the feast was to last for three days! On the first day, the Indians did nothing but eat, but later on, they wrestled, ran races, sang and danced with the young people in the colony. They could outrun and outwrestle the boys, but on the other hand, they learned some new games and loved marching to the rhythm of a drum. They were more than frightened when someone fired a cannon!

Thanksgiving Today

Thanksgiving is, almost without exception, the family's day. Christmas or New Year's Day may be spent with friends, but

Thanksgiving dinners are family affairs and celebrated almost entirely within the home. One fine way in which the people celebrate Thanksgiving is to attend a church service in the morning and in many localities, persons of different faith worship together. It is also a time of sharing with the less fortunate, and churches, schools and many philanthropic societies see to it that no one goes hungry. To many, it is the one day in the year they remember to give thanks for all America has done for them.

Family Party Entertainment

Since Thanksgiving Day is more or less the "gathering of the clan," there will be all ages – grandparents, parents and little children–seated in the family circle. It is a good idea to start the entertainment at the dinner table and provide fun in which all can participate while the meal is being served. For one thing–if the family is inclined to sing, there are many good table songs. It might be well to type the words ahead of time so each person can have a copy. Here are a few appropriate titles:

Home themes	*Rustic themes*
Home Sweet Home	Coming Through the Rye
Home on the Range	Old Oaken Bucket
My Old Kentucky Home	Bringing in the Sheaves
Seeing Nellie Home	Crackin' Corn

And here are some table games that have to do with the family. You might start off by handing each person a piece of paper on which the following is written:

My Family Tree

My sister's daughter is my—(niece),
Her uncle is my—(brother),
And his grandfather's son's wife
Happens to be my—(mother).

My mother's sister is my—(aunt),
And her son is my—(cousin),
That's the kind of relative,
That I have by the dozen.

My cousin's father is my—(uncle),
His brother is my—(father),
I wonder if a family tree,
Is really worth the bother.

If you want the relationships a bit more complicated, try this one:
Your father's uncle's brother's sister—(great-aunt)
Your aunt's mother's father's wife—(great-grandmother)
Your mother's nephew's daughter's son—(third cousin)
Your brother's son's sister's mother—(sister-in-law)
Your sister-in-law's father-in-law's grandson—(nephew)
Your sister's father's stepson's mother—(stepmother)
Your uncle's father's only grandchild—(yourself)
Your brother-in-law's wife's grandmother's husband—(grandfather)

Family Jokes—Most families derive great amusement from jokes on each other, and the suggestion that everyone tell a joke will be received with enthusiasm. If need be—recall some famous family jokes that might not be familiar to everyone present.

Family History—For the purpose of testing the general knowledge of the family history, provide each person with a list of dates on which have occurred events of interest to the family in general. These might include birthdays, wedding anniversaries, graduations, changes in moving or residence, etc.

Family Secrets—This last game should be enacted as a charade.

Let different members leave the table and act out a secret of some kind for the rest of the family to guess. Once the family secrets start to come out, there will be no stopping them. They may have to do with pet peeves, secret dates, future plans, etc. To keep the occasion happy, be kind to persons who are sensitive and less charitable, if you like, to ones who have a sense of humor.

After-Dinner Entertainment

Folk games that have come down through the ages and ones that originated with home festivals are familiar to most children. They include Farmer in the Dell, Jolly Miller, Blind man's Buff, etc. For children who like to act or are creative, we would like to suggest:

Tableaux

This form of entertainment requires no props if you have an archway between two rooms—if not, a large wooden frame will serve the purpose. The characters in the tableau will require some costuming and if the children do not have access to old clothes, suggestive accessories made of paper will do as well.

Since a tableau is a living picture represented by one or more silent and motionless characters, we would like to offer the following suggestions:

A sheet can serve as a curtain while the tableau is being formed. Let two children hold it in place as shown in the illustration.

Have an announcer to tell about the picture before the curtain falls free from the door. On the other hand, the tableau may be in the form of a charade, where the audience must guess the subject.

Never stand directly in front of another character. The important people should be in front; but they must never entirely hide one of the others; every part of the picture counts.

If you wish the tableau to seem real, you must pretend that you are really the person you represent.

Suggested Subjects for Tableaux

Thanksgiving Long Ago	Thanksgiving Today
First Thanksgiving	The Pilgrims Going to Church
Pilgrim Fathers	Family Portraits

Fun with Vegetables

Place a basket of fruit and vegetables on a table along with a package of construction paper, transparent Scotch tape, scissors and toothpicks. Suggest that children use their imagination and make animals for a barnyard or zoo, or hand puppets if they prefer.

Vegetable Animals

Here are some examples of animals made from vegetables. The features are cut from construction paper and held in place with Scotch tape. Toothpicks or matches serve as legs.

Vegetable Candy

Candy made in the form of fruits and vegetables is traditionally known as "Marzipan" and is a favorite sweet served at all festivals.

Mix together—

½ pound of confectioner's sugar
6 ounces finely ground almonds
1 unbeaten egg

Combine the ingredients with a knife, knead well and set aside for an hour. Mold into fruit shapes and tint with vegetable coloring. This is done with a brush, and when the fruit is dry, add an artificial stem or foliage.

Puppets for a Day

Fruits or vegetables can be used for puppet heads and provide plenty of amusement for children all Thanksgiving afternoon. The body is made from a square piece of cloth. Find the center of the square and cut a hole large enough to insert the index finger, and two other holes for the thumb and middle finger to come through. Now hollow out the inside of an apple or vegetable for a head, being careful to make the hole just large enough to insert the index finger. Form the features with a knife or thumbtacks.

Turnip Puppets

These little puppets are made from white turnips. If the head is made with the root on top, it makes a kewpie-like face. If it is reversed, with the root hanging down, the effect will be an old man with a beard.

Corncob Doll

Colonial children played with dolls made from corncobs. Paint a face on the large end of the cob and add some corn silks for hair. Dress it in a doll's costume, or just wrap the lower part of the corncob in a shawl.

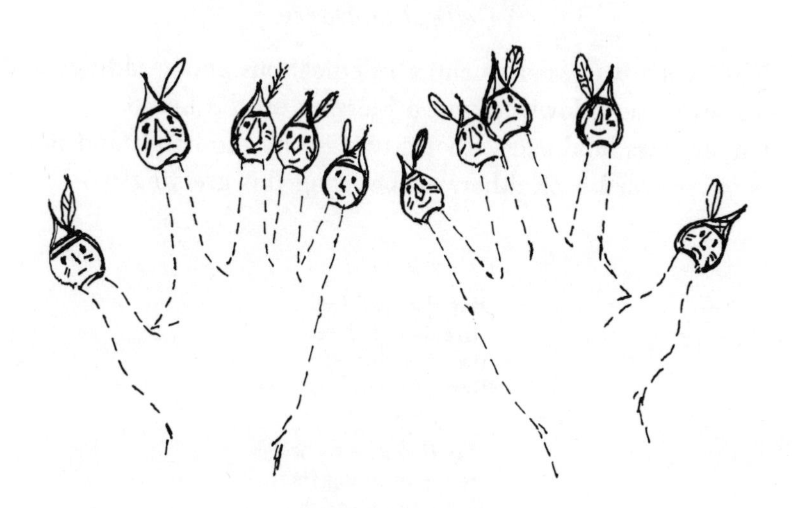

Ten Little Indians (Finger Play)

Each little Indian is a radish hollowed out enough in the center to fit over a finger. Add a feather at the top and paint on some features. At the beginning, have only one Indian showing—then match the number mentioned in the song as it goes up or down the scale.

A Dedication Dance

This dance was used at church dedications and weddings and expresses close fellowship and a blessing on the house.

The dancers hold each other crosswise by the hands and move solemnly toward each other, as they sing this greeting:

May the Lord God
Give us His love,
Our sins forgive,
Grant us Heaven,
Also.
May God give us health
As we dwell together,
God give us health.
Give us health.

Thanksgiving Parades

As far back as history reaches the Festival of Harvest Home, which became our Thanksgiving, was marked by picturesque parades of happy people bearing the first fruits or grain through the streets in honor of the gods who foster crops. Sometimes, a rustic maiden called the "harvest queen" rode in on one of the horses that brought in the last sheath of grain that was bedecked with ribbons and flowers. The Romans, also, had fantastic parades in honor of the last wagon in from the field and the harvesters contended in all kinds of games and sports.

In the United States, many Thanksgiving parades take place, but any connotation to a harvest festival is lost. Some are patriotic in character, but the more spectacular ones are commercial and are sponsored by large department stores in large cities. Among the most notable ones that are usually televised are:

Macy's Thanksgiving Parade

Macy's Department Store in New York City has held a famous Thanksgiving parade since 1924. The parade begins at 77th Street and Central Park West about 10 A.M. and moves down Broadway, ending about noon in front of the store at 34th Street. The parade is most spectacular, with tremendous helium-inflated images of storybook and comic-book characters. The large balloons average about 6,000 cubic feet in size—some are 50-60 feet long and taller than some of the buildings along the streets. Other regular features are floats depicting fairy stories, a dozen bands and a big showboat. As many as 2,500,000 persons witness the spectacle.

Gimbel Brothers Parade

Gimbel Brothers' store in Philadelphia holds a parade on Thanksgiving Day. It is called "Uncle Whip," named after the store's Uncle Whip, who glorifies toyland and characters from juvenile fiction. It is more or less a preview of toys for Christmas trade.

Plymouth, Massachusetts

The people of Plymouth, Massachusetts, reenact the first American Thanksgiving each year. Dressed in colonial costumes, they gather at the famous rock and bow their heads in gratitude. Then, with men carrying old-fashioned muskets, the crowd marches to Burial Hill, where Pilgrims who died that first winter are buried. From there, they go to Memorial Hall to hear a Thanksgiving sermon delivered by one of the local ministers.

Thanksgiving Day Festival in California

One of the most noteworthy Thanksgiving festivals is held each year at Pilgrim Place, Claremont, California. It is a community made up of retired ministers, doctors, missionaries and other Christian workers—some of whom claim to be descendants of Mayflower passengers. In order to earn funds for community projects, it has been their custom since 1949 to hold a two-day Thanksgiving festival which is a combination of pageantry and money-making devices.

The men wear Puritan attire, including tall hats and buckles on their shoes, while women wear typical colonial costumes. The bazaar consists of booths filled with articles made by the sponsors; children can be photographed in stocks and there is a replica of the *Mayflower* on wheels. A pageant, *Pilgrim's Triumphs,* is staged each night. It depicts their life from the time they left their homeland, their journey by sea, and the first Thanksgiving in America.

12. CHRISTMAS

In all the year, there is no day that fills the heart of the world with so much joy as Christmas. Since the most ancient times, people of all races have held festivals or feast days on which they ate, drank and made merry—generally in honor of their gods. Thus, in many lands this Christmas festival is interwoven with ancient folklore and legends that have been handed down from generation to generation, even to the present time.

Christmas is the most important festival in Christian countries, celebrating the birth of Christ, and people express their joy and devotion in many different ways. In this chapter, we have sorted out a number of ancient legends and customs that can be adapted for use in modern Christmas pageants, church and school programs, community celebrations, or for parties in the home.

The Many Moods of American Christmas

Our United States are scattered across a vast territory, inhabited by people from all sections of Europe and Asia, and Christmas comes to each of them with different traditions. Could we be in all places at once on Christmas Eve, we would surely stop suddenly and say, "Is this our country after all?"

To start on the Atlantic seaboard, where our nation began, in New England villages bands of carolers, ringing hand bells, lift

their voices on Christmas Eve. It is fitting that the early celebrations in Virginia, and generally throughout the South, should be represented by an annual celebration in new-born Williamsburg. There, as in colonial days, the yule log is brought in and lit with ancient ceremony in a setting that George Washington and Thomas Jefferson would have found familiar.

In Philadelphia are descendants of Swedish settlers and the legend of Saint Lucia with her candlelighted wreath of leaves, is recalled. If we go a little farther into Pennsylvania, we would see the old customs of the Pennsylvania Dutch with the elaborate construction of the Putz (the Christmas crib), including a whole landscape of sheep, camels and buildings, with a tree quite subordinated.

If we could visit the South, we would find the day not only warm, but the night air would be filled with fireworks. Christmas Day is a family day in New Orleans, as in France, and crèches are carefully erected, even in the smallest homes.

California boasts of having the most elaborate Christmas festival, which is staged in a most spectacular location—the Yosemite National Park. Here, one of the great hotels produces a dramatic spectacle. While dusk is falling over the tall trees in the park, bands of men dressed in white-caped and cowled costumes to represent the ancient Druids, gather from all directions, wending their way toward the celebration along different trails, plainly visible in the dark forest. They enter the age-old hotel chanting melodies and bearing with them an enormous yule log, covered with mistletoe, which they have brought from the forest. It is placed with ceremony into the great fireplace and lighted with a brand that has been treasured from the log of the year before.

The following night, the remnants of the yule log are taken up a steep slope and laid on a fire built at Glacier Point, high above the valley. Then, just as the light fades from the western sky, the fire is pushed from this point to become a flaming fireball that hisses and streaks down a mountainside to a ledge of rocks hundreds of feet below.

Thus, at the edge of the Pacific, ends the American Christmas Day which had begun with caroling to the chimes of hand bells in the circular streets of Boston, on the Atlantic seaboard, just twenty-four hours before.

Christmas Legends and Customs

Nothing says Christmas more directly or more exuberantly than folk customs—a well of inspiration that never runs dry. It is true that we have borrowed much of our seasonal regalia from other lands, but how many know from where they sprang, or their true significance? Many have to do with symbolism, mixed with legends of ancient origins, and we have endeavored to select ones that might contribute to an international theme or just a plain Christmas celebration.

The Christmas Tree

There are many legends, indeed, concerning the origin of the Christmas tree. The first Christmas tree mentioned in literature was in Strasbourg in 1604, but the one associated with Martin Luther is the most familiar. It is related that he wandered through the woods one starry Christmas Eve and became enamored of the wonders of the night, for the sky was filled with stars. He cut a small snow-laden fir tree and, when he returned home, set it up for his children and illuminated it with numerous candles to represent the stars.

Another legend, a much more ancient one, tells how in the eighteenth century, St. Boniface persuaded the Teutons to give up their cruel practice of sacrificing a child before a great oak tree during their midwinter festival. Instead, he said, "Cut down a big fir tree, take it home, and celebrate around it with your innocent children." He also told them that the fir was the wood of peace, from which their houses were built, that it was a sign of immortality, because its leaves were ever green and its top branches pointed straight to heaven.

The Word Xmas

Contrary to the common misconception that Xmas is an abbreviation for Christmas, it is a definite word and not one devised by laziness.

The use of "X" to stand for Christmas began in the early days of Christianity when persecution drove the believers underground, literally, in Rome. The cult was forced to take on the aspects of a secret society. "X" was considered a reverent sign because it was a reminder of the cross on which Christ was crucified.

The Steaua

In Romania, boys go from house to house singing carols, reciting poetry and legend during the Christmas season. The leader of the group carries a large wooden star called a "Steaua." It is covered with gilt paper and adorned with bells and frills of colored ribbons. A picture of the Holy Family is painted or pasted in the center, which is illuminated with a candle. The whole is attached to the top of a stout pole, such as the handle of a broomstick.

American carolers might enjoy making a Steaua and carrying it at the head of a group as they go about singing on Christmas Eve. It would add color and distinction to the group.

The Piñata

This is the part of Christmas Mexican children like best of all. A piñata is a fragile earthern jar made especially to hold toys and favors. Piñatas are gaily decorated; some look like clowns or very fat people, some have roses, stars, or other Christmas symbols. They are suspended from the ceiling or, more often, hung in the doorway of a room.

The children form a circle around the piñata and put one of their number in the center with his eyes blindfolded. He is given a stick and permitted three tries at breaking it. The other children, meanwhile, sing and dance around in a circle. If the first child does not succeed in breaking the jar, another child tries. When the piñata is broken, causing a shower of gifts to pour down onto the floor, the entire party makes a wild scramble to obtain their share.

Sometimes three piñatas are hung in the room. One is filled with water; another with confetti; another with gifts, sweets and fruits—this is the good piñata.

Julklapp

In Denmark and Holland, before Christmas Day arrives, all presents intended for the Julklapp delivery must be prepared and wrapped by enclosing them in a great many wrappings of various kinds. None should suggest the contents in any way. The follow-

JENNY LIND AND HER CHRISTMAS TREE

ing description portrays the time and effort this custom consumes:

If one of the presents is a trinket, wrap it up in fringed paper such as is used for candy or sugar kisses; place it in a small box, tie the box with a narrow ribbon; then do it up in common brown paper and wrap the package with strips of cloth until it is round like a ball. Cover this with a layer of dough and brown in the oven. Finally, pin it up in a napkin, wrap it in white wrapping paper, and tie with a pink string.

Jenny Lind's Christmas in America

Jenny Lind spent her first Christmas in this country in Charleston, South Carolina, in 1851, and Laura Benét in her book, *Enchanting Jenny Lind*, gives a delightful description of her gifts to her associates with the Julklapp-like wrappings and the fun that ensued.

Jenny Lind had never seen any place like it, and the old, childlike joy bubbled up in her. She resolved to keep Christmas in her own Swedish way since her first concert was put off until the day after Christmas. Busying both herself and her staff with the purchase of a huge Christmas tree, she had it set up in her apartment and carefully trimmed. Presents for every one of her company and servants hung from its branches, labelled and ready for Christmas Eve. The smell of pine and freshly baked cakes filled the rooms. Charleston was ransacked for any trifles that would be amusing, and the relaxed prima donna smiled and played and was a happy child again. She invited the whole troupe to come to a party on Christmas Eve. When the tree was lighted, the doors were thrown open, and all of them were ushered in. "A strict lady of the court might have objected to the frank eagerness with which she seated her company like a schoolgirl preparing her playfellows for a game at forfeits; but it was charming to those who were made at home by it." Delightful jokes had been carefully done up and were impressively presented.

"Jules Benedict, this is for you," and Jenny took down a huge package from the tree. "Mr. Barnum, you come next"—and she read a label. "Here is something you will fancy." A heavy, weighty object was put carefully into her manager's arms: "Take care now of the child. It may break to pieces"—and her eyes danced.

"Giovanni," she continued, "this tiny packet of sweetmeats contains a very costly object." (She knew the Italian had a sweet tooth.) The "costly object" was a gilt ring. And the distribution went on, gaily.

Jules Benedict, her pianist, took forty layers of paper from a huge parcel, unwrapping diligently while the group watched him in great amusement. Finally at the end, under the numerous layers he found a small, white morsel—and snatched at it. It was an envelope in which was *one* piece of Cavendish tobacco!

Mr. Barnum had also taken the wrappings from his gift. "See," he said, *"Bacchus!,"* and he waved around his head a little statuette of the god of wine in Parian marble, a challenge to his temperance principles. Soon all was laughter and jollity. . . Every one joined in the mirth of an old-fashioned Christmas Eve; there were real presents as well as jokes and each seemed to receive just what he wanted.

The Ceppo

In Italy, the Ceppo is equivalent to our Christmas tree. It is made with a framework of lath-like strips of wood with three or four shelves, graduating in size as shown in the illustration. If it is to be a permanent structure, make the shelves of three-ply wood, otherwise, heavy cardboard will suffice. Paint the Ceppo with several colors of paint and add tufts and tassels along the sides. The Italians further ornament it with tiny pine cones and candles along the edges and place a much larger cone or a puppet at the top.

Generally, each child has his own Ceppo. The upper shelves are used to hold gifts and some are laden with candy and nuts. On the bottom shelf is placed the infant Jesus, surrounded by shepherds, saints and angels.

A Ceppo built on a larger scale would make a novel arrangement for gifts for the whole family.

A Shoe for St. Nicholas

In the St. Nicholas countries, on the sixth of December, the children place their shoes outside the window, hoping St. Nicholas will drive by with gifts for good boys and girls. He rides about on a white horse, followed by a cart laden with parcels to be left at the different houses. Before they go to sleep, the children stuff their shoes with hay and place a saucer of water beside them, so the horse will have something to eat during the journey. By the same token, American children might fill their shoes with food for Santa's reindeers.

Christmas in Poland

In Poland, Christmas dinner is served in the evening, just as the evening star appears in the winter sky. The meal consists of twelve courses—one for each Apostle. They have a saying, "Our hearts are open to stranger, kith and kin," so one empty seat is always left at the table in case an unknown traveler should appear to share the meal.

Christmas Birds

In Scandinavian countries no one is ever forgotten. Even the animals in the barn receive extra rations and a sheaf of wheat, dipped in suet, is hung in the crisp cold outside so the birds, too, will have their Christmas. It is usually fastened to a long pole which stands in the middle of the dooryard. There is not a peasant in all Sweden who will sit down with his children until he has first raised aloft a Christmas dinner for the little birds that live in the snow.

Christmas Star

Christmas, with its blazing glory of neon lights along the main thoroughfare of most American towns, has the brightest light of all on the highest building—the Christmas Star. It is symbolic of the manifestation of the birth of Jesus and the journey of the Three Wise Men to Bethlehem. For the same reason, a gold star is placed at the top of a Christmas tree.

Layette Night

Layette Night is observed in France on Christmas Eve. It is the custom for women to gather together to make layettes, not only for friends who are expectant mothers, but others to be distributed to the poor on Christmas morning.

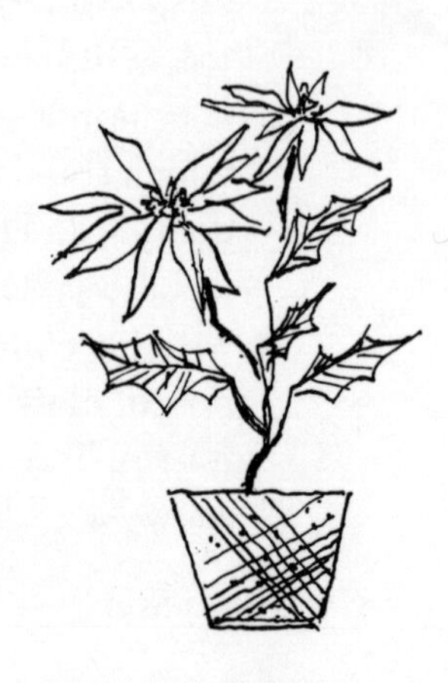

CHRISTMAS GREENS AND THEIR MEANING

Poinsettia

Along with the fir, holly and mistletoe, the Poinsettia has become a traditional Christmas decoration. Indeed, it has virtually become a symbol of Christmas with its crimson, star-shaped flower. It was brought to this country one hundred twenty-five years ago by Dr. Joel Poinsett and is still called by many "Flor de Noche Buena"—the Flower of the Holy Night.

There are many legends surrounding this, nature's Christmas-colored wonder. One tale related how a poor Mexican girl was heartbroken because she had nothing of value or beauty to offer the Virgin. In desperation, she plucked some scrawny roadside weeds and placed them at the feet of the holy statue. They were immediately transformed into the scarlet brilliance of the poinsettia.

Mistletoe

"These are bright eyes that sparkle so
When whispered neath the mistletoe
'a kiss we'll seal'."

Mistletoe was the sacred plant of the Druids, and once a year, five days after the first new moon, men, women and children stood under the oak tree that bore the most mistletoe. First came the bards and then a herald to hail it with loud shouts of delight and reverence. Then came the arch-Druid dressed in a white robe; gold bands were around his arms and a gold chain about his neck. He ascended the tree and with a gold sickle, cut away the lowest bough on which the mistletoe was growing. The priest then broke the branches into many pieces and gave a twig to each of his followers with a prayer "that each who received a branch should find divine favor and a blessing from nature." Because of its heathen origin, many churches will not sanction the mistletoe as a decoration in a religious edifice.

The lassies who get kissed under the mistletoe have an old

Scandinavian myth to thank for this charming custom. It was the goddess Frigga who hung mistletoe high and was first to stand under the glistening white berries offering kisses to all who passed beneath it.

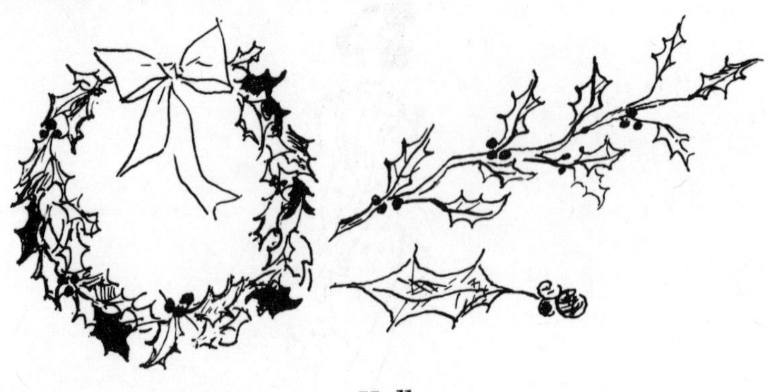

Holly

Holly was worshiped before the birth of Christ by people who considered the greenness in the middle of the winter as a promise of the sun's return in another year. The early French and English hung sprigs of the bright-berried plant on their doors to indicate homes in which Christ dwelled. According to some sources, Christ's crown of thorns had been fashioned from holly leaves. At first its berries were white, but when the crown was pressed down on His brow, blood drops turned the berries bright red.

Ivy

The ivy and holly are often associated together in legends—the holly is male because of its sturdiness and the ivy as feminine and clinging. A fifteenth-century carol tells of a contest between the Holly and the Ivy for the place of honor in the hall. It is in the form of a duet given as follows:

Contest of the Ivy and the Holly

CHORUS

Nay, Ivy, nay, it shall not be, I wis,
Let Holly have the mastery as the manner is.

Holly standeth in the hall fair to behold,
Ivy standeth without the door; she is full sore a cold.
Nay, Ivy, nay, etc.
Holly and his merry men, they dancin and they sing;
Ivy and her maidens, they weepen and they ring.
Nay, Ivy, nay, etc.
Ivy hath a lylie, she caught it with the cold,
So may they all have, that with Ivy hold.
Nay, Ivy, nay, etc.
Holly hath berries as red as any rose,
The foresters, the hunters, keep them from the does.
Nay, Ivy, nay, etc.
Ivy hath berries as black as any sloe,
There come the owl and eat them as she go.
Nay, Ivy, nay, etc.
Holly hath birds a full fair flock,
The nightingale, the poppinjay, the gentle laverock.
Nay, Ivy, nay, etc.
Good Ivy (good ivy) what birds hast thou,
None but the owlet that cries, "How! How."
Nay, Ivy, nay, etc.

FROM MANUSCRIPT OF HENRY IV'S TIME

The Holly and the Ivy

The holly and the ivy
Now are both well grown,
Of all the trees that are in the wood
The holly bears the crown.

CHORUS

The rising of the sun,
The running of the deer,
The playing of the merry organ,
The singing in the choir.
The holly bears a blossom
As white as any flower,
And Mary bore sweet Jesus Christ
To be our sweet Savior.
The holly bears a berry
As red as any blood,
And Mary bore sweet Jesus Christ
To do poor sinners good.
The holly bears a prickle
As sharp as any thorn,
And Mary bore sweet Jesus Christ
On Christmas day in the morn.
The holly bears a bark
As bitter as any gall,
And Mary bore sweet Jesus Christ
For to redeem us all.
The holly and the ivy
Now are both well grown,
Of all the trees that are in the wood
The holly bears the crown.

Printed about 1710.

TRADITIONAL DECORATIONS

Garlands

According to the dictionary, a garland is a "wreath," but we think of it as a long strand decorated in the round with leaves or flowers. In the North, laurel or holly leaves are preferred, while the southerners make garlands, not only of holly, but of pine and oak leaves as well.

In order to make a garland, a central stem of some kind must be used, such as heavy string or rope, for attaching the greens. To make a garland or wreath look professional, all flowers and fruits should be wired, not only to hold them in place, but so they can be bent in different directions. Also, there must be a contrast in forms and colors between the leaves in order to have an interesting arrangement.

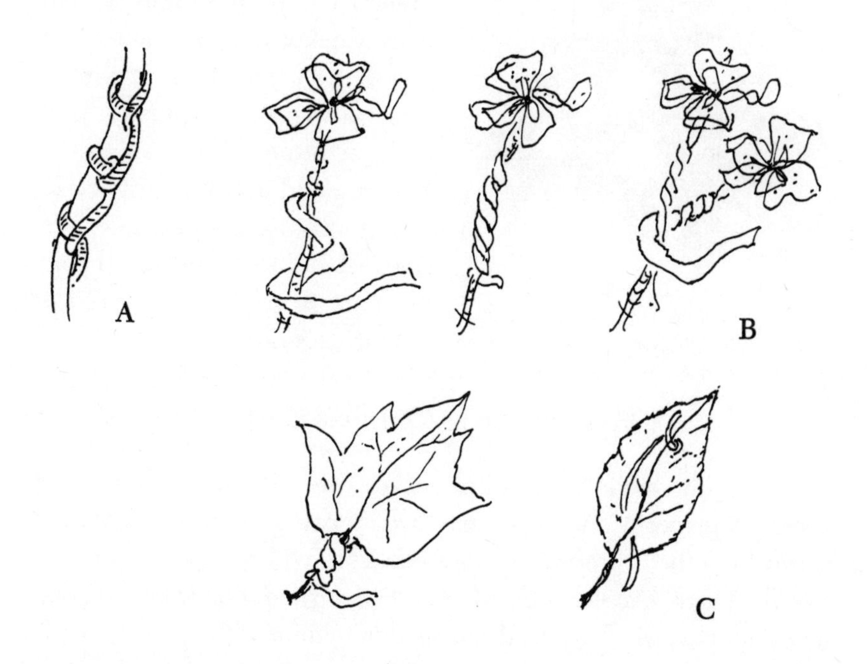

Several methods are used for attaching ornaments to the central stem, according to their size and weight:

A – To make a garland of flowers, wrap each stem with green tissue paper the length of the flower, then add them one by one as shown in the figure above.

B – Greens can be added to a central stem by tying them in place with half hitches.

C – To wire the ornaments, use the thinnest wire possible and cut it into lengths a little longer than you think you will need. If the ornaments are heavy, the wire must be wrapped around the center strand at least twice.

A Kissing Bough

A large branch of pine or bough of a tree covered with holly is a gay variation of the mistletoe. Most attractive are the ones made from a well-shaped branch cut from a tree—be sure it is thicker in the center. To give it a deeper sense of dimension, cover it completely with holly or other Christmas greens. You can add a number of scarlet Christmas balls—spangled versions of nature's berries. It may be hung in the room or used as a door decoration.

How to Preserve Christmas Greens

Stems that have large, thick leaves are put into a solution of one part glycerin and two parts water. Allow them to remain in it until all the water is evaporated. This will take three or four weeks. Thick leaves, such as laurel and rhododendron, are particularly successful when dried in this manner.

Candles

In Ireland, candles are lighted and placed in windows on Christmas Eve to light the Christ Child on His way. This custom of burning candles on Christmas Eve has remained constant. During many centuries in England and France, the yule candle was of enormous size and large holes were chiseled in the stone floors to act as holders. On Christmas, the dinner lasted as long as the candle burned.

In some countries in Europe, three candles are placed at the top of a Christmas tree, symbolizing the Trinity.

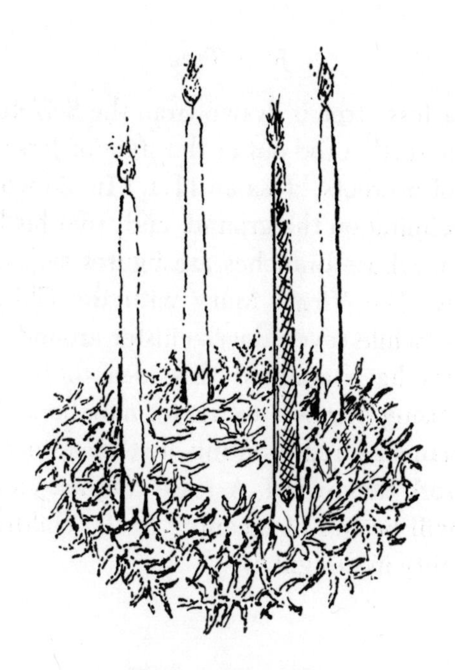

Advent Wreath

The wreath, an old Christian custom originating in Germany several centuries ago, is simply a circle of greenery around which four candles—one for each week of Advent (four weeks before Christmas)—are equally spaced. They are lavender, symbolizing the penitence of the season. You may make a base of wood with permanent candleholders, or buy your wreath already made and add the candles.

Make the wreath the center of attraction in your home, in the dining room, the children's room, or in a large hallway. Each Sunday gather the children together to say a short prayer or read a verse from Scripture. One candle is lighted the first Sunday and an additional one each week thereafter until on Christmas Eve the wreath is a glowing testament to the nearness of the Savior. You may make one of the four candles pink to symbolize the joy of Gaudete Sunday (third Sunday of Advent) or on Christmas Eve make it a part of your holiday decorations by using all red candles.

Jesse Tree

The idea of a Jesse tree is drawn from the Scriptural text, "And there shall come forth a rod out of the stem of Jesse, and a branch shall grow out of his roots." (Isaiah 11:1.) In old world cathedrals, Jesse is seen reclining on the ground, and from his body springs a stylized tree, on whose branches are figures symbolizing the ancestors of Jesus. The Virgin Mary with the Child in her arms crowns the tree, while seven doves cluster around.

Many families have adapted this idea to the making of an ancestral tree, using symbols to depict members of each generation. Place ornaments representing first ancestors at the top of the tree and work downward. A Jesse tree may not be showy or gaudy, but it will be full of meaning to the children and a challenge to originality in design!

MAKE MERRY WITH AN OLD-FASHIONED CHRISTMAS

Many of us approach the holiday season with mixed emotions —straining the imagination for ways to increase some measure of originality in our entertainment. Since Christmas is truly a festival holiday, why not plan at least one party in the spirit of "An Old-Fashioned Christmas." Even though your friends take a dim view of old-fashioned customs and traditions, they will be imbued with the Christmas season when they see the yule log being brought in ceremoniously, the wassail bowl steaming with fluffy liquid and carolers singing joyously.

Most of our practiced customs come from England, but it is easy to find one from other countries by consulting books in the library or asking people of foreign birth. An excellent idea is to get a catalogue of recordings for listings of Christmas music, dances and, perhaps, readings from Dickens' "Christmas Carol" or other stories. We have selected the following activities that should fit into any Christmas festival, be it in the home, church or community:

The Yule Log

If you are fortunate enough to have a fireplace, the bringing in of the yule log is a favorite Christmas celebration in our northern states. The choppers meet on the village square and, after a round of carol singing, they head to the woods to search for the yule log which was notched and hidden there weeks before. It is decorated with evergreens and hauled to its destination with great pomp and ceremony, where it is lighted with a brand saved from last year's log. The master of the house does the hauling, assisted by the eldest son, while the youngest of the family rides atop. The father then offers a prayer that the fire might warm the cold, that the hungry might gain food, that the weary find rest, and that all enjoy heaven's peace.

A Basket of Fagots

A welcome change of pace to a Christmas party is to gather around the fireplace for a period of good conversation. A basket of fagots, arranged ahead of time, can add merriment to the group if used in the traditional manner:

Each guest is given a little bundle of sticks, tied together with a supple twig, and each, in turn, places it on the fire and tells a story. Its length depends on the time required to reduce the fagots to ashes.

Another traditional use of the fagots is to tie a number of sticks into a bundle with nine supple bands of bark. It is placed on the fire Christmas night and each girl in the company chooses a band. The first to burn indicates the girl who will be first to marry. It is the duty of the host to pass to each guest a mug of cider or ale saying, "When the green bands that bindeth the fagots do burst, it is time, good people, to have a drink and wish everybody well."

Games

Old Christmas games are the very familiar ones such as Blind Man's Buff, Forfeits, Hunt the Slipper, etc. These will satisfy very young children, but if your guests are older, you must plan something different. Some popular games have rules that can be adapted to a Christmas theme with holiday symbols for properties, or you can divide the guests into groups and give each a name such as Holly and Ivy, Baubles and Wreaths or, if you want to include food, Sugar Plums and Candy Canes.

Snapdragon

One of the oldest Christmas games is called "Snapdragon." A quantity of raisins are put into a large, shallow bowl with brandy or some other spirit poured over it and the fruit ignited. The bystanders endeavor, in turn, to grasp a raisin by plunging their hands through the flames. It is usual to turn out all lights in the room to give a weird effect.

Christmas Notes

Italy has a charming custom that is practiced on Christmas Day. The children write letters or poems expressing their love and appreciation of their fathers and mothers during the past year. Before the Christmas dinner, they hide their literary efforts somewhere on the table. They may be tucked into a napkin, under a plate, or even under the tablecloth. Parents pretend not to see them until the meal is almost over. Then they are discovered with a show of great surprise, and read aloud to the delight of all the family.

Christmas Yule

To play this game, divide a holly branch in two and ask a friend to "Yule" with you during the evening. If she consents, you give her one of the pieces of holly. After this, you must be careful not to take anything from her hands for, if you do, she will instantly exclaim "Yule" and you will have to give her whatever you agreed on previously. If, however, you can get her to take anything from you, you exclaim "Yule" and it is you who wins.

This can go on for several days. You must be ready to show your "Yule" at all times, or you will loose your wager.

Christmas Pieces

Christmas "Pieces" were specimens of handwriting, carefully prepared under the supervision of the writing master, in all English schools immediately before breakup to go home for the holidays. They were to manifest to the parents and guardians the improvement made during the year by the pupil. They were bordered by engravings, the space in the center being reserved for the writing.

Christmas and Easter—A Singing Game

Words:

1. Now 'tis Christmas time, now 'tis Christmas time,
   And Christmas time will last till Easter;
2. Now 'tis Easter time, now 'tis Easter time,
   And Easter time will last till Christmas.

Formation:

Couples in sets of four abreast facing other fours at about ten feet. Sets are numbered one or two.

Step:

A light running step.

Action:

1. Set Number One, run forward 6 steps and back 5 steps, during the words "Now 'tis Christmas time, now 'tis Christmas time, and Christmas time will last till Easter."
2. Same is repeated by set Number Two.
1. Each set of four does a circle to the left (12 counts – turn on word "Easter").
2. Each set of four, circle to right.
1. Each set of eight (one set Number One and opposite set Number Two) circle left as above.
2. The circle is repeated to right.
1. Each set of four forms a pinwheel with right hands joined, move clockwise, 12 steps.

2. Each set of four repeats the pinwheel with left hands joined, move counterclockwise 12 steps.
1. Repeat with pinwheel of eight, ladies form pinwheel, men walk beside partners, arms linked.
2. All face about, repeat with ladies' left hands joined.
1. and (2) repeated indefinitely.

   Weaving. First player of each top set now leads his set with hands joined around behind the second set, in front of the third, and so on, making a loop at the end of the line, and coming to rest at end of line, in the same order as at the start. This leaves a new top set.

Repeat from very beginning until all sets have been at top.

(Reprinted from *Musical Mixers and Simple Square Dances* by courtesy of the National Recreation Association, 315 Fourth Avenue, N. Y.)

The Christmas Tree

The tree is still the oldest and most celebrated symbol of the Christmas season. Every year, Americans spend about fifty million dollars for Christmas trees plus a few million more for baubles, so it can be labeled "big business." Recently, this honored symbol has become an unbelievable swaggering array of lights and balls which overshadow the true meaning of yesteryear. Any decoration, modest or magnificent, grows twice its size in sentiment when it emerges a true Christmas symbol.

Of course, it is possible to buy Christmas tree ornaments of all descriptions, but it is more fun to make them as part of the holiday preparations. The children will enjoy making little trinkets like their grandmother made, not to mention stringing popcorn, paper chains, cornets, etc. Here are a few very simple ones that seem to have been discarded as the years passed by:

Cornucopia

This is the horn of plenty originally used by the Greeks as a decoration. It symbolizes the goddess Amalthea who was endowed with the virtue of becoming filled with whatever the possessor

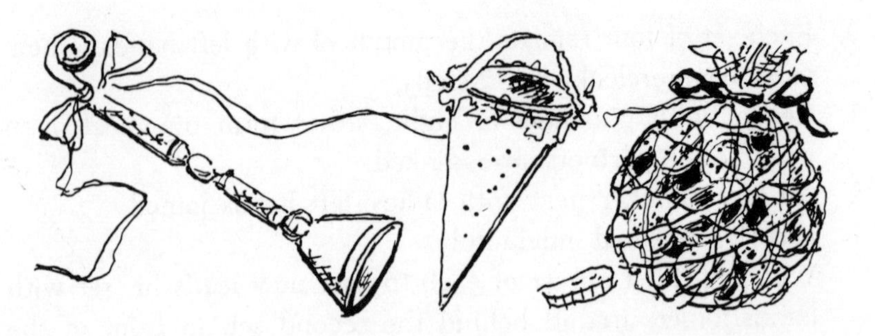

wished. The cone is usually filled to overflowing, depicting an inexhaustible supply.

Cornets

A cornet is a piece of paper rolled into the shape of a cone and twisted at the top. It is used for wrapping small packages or containers for nuts and miniature candies. A gold foil gives best results and is more in keeping with the original design.

Open Mesh Containers

Baglike containers were made of coarse, open mesh for the purpose of holding trinkets and candy and allowing the color to shine through. They were usually in the form of Santa Claus, a drawstring bag, or a stocking. They were made by cutting out two pieces of net the same size and shape and binding them together with red or green bias tape.

Popcorn

Children love to make long strips of popcorn and use them as garlands on their Christmas tree. Another use for popcorn is to run pins through individual kernels, then attach them to the ends of each twig on the tree by forcing in the point of the pin. This makes the tree sparkle and gives the effect of snow.

Christmas Doll or Angel

Many families place a tiny doll or angel near the top of a Christmas tree, just below the star. After the presents are opened on Christmas Day, all draw lots for possession of the doll for the coming year. It must be returned in time to be hung on the next year's tree.

Decorated Cookies

The custom of hanging cookies on a Christmas tree is an age-old one. The cookies may be decorated a number of ways—a Christmas scene pasted on the front (use icing for paste), ornamented with colored frosting, or cut into shapes of a Christmas symbol, such as Santa Claus, tree, star, stocking, etc.

Gewgaws

Gewgaws are gaudy trifles, of little value, used to give color and sparkle to a Christmas tree. Making them is no problem today, with an abundance of multicolored metallic paper, costume jewelry, pocket mirrors, miniature trinkets, etc., but they were quite a challenge to our grandmothers! We have rummaged through some boxes of old Christmas tree decorations and come up with the ones illustrated on page 176, which really need no explanation as how to make them. Anyway, here are a few hints:

Snappers. To most people today, a four- or five-inch tube wrapped in a gaily colored paper and fringed at each end where it is tied is a "party snapper." Not so in Grandma's time – the package was much smaller, and inside was an oblong piece of candy.

Gilded Nuts. It was the custom, when nuts were a luxury item, to gild them with gold or silver paint and hang them on the Christmas tree. Sometimes English walnuts were broken in half, the kernel removed, and then hinged together on one side so they could be opened or closed. Inside would be a verse of some kind or a tiny Nativity scene.

Birds of all kinds were made of paper or cardboard and then painted in many colors. Sometimes the birds were made of yarn.

Old Toys were kept from year to year and hung on the Christmas tree. Underneath the tree might be Grandfather's hobbyhorse, tin soldiers, a ball, a top, an iron money bank, a red engine, etc.—a beautiful custom, really!

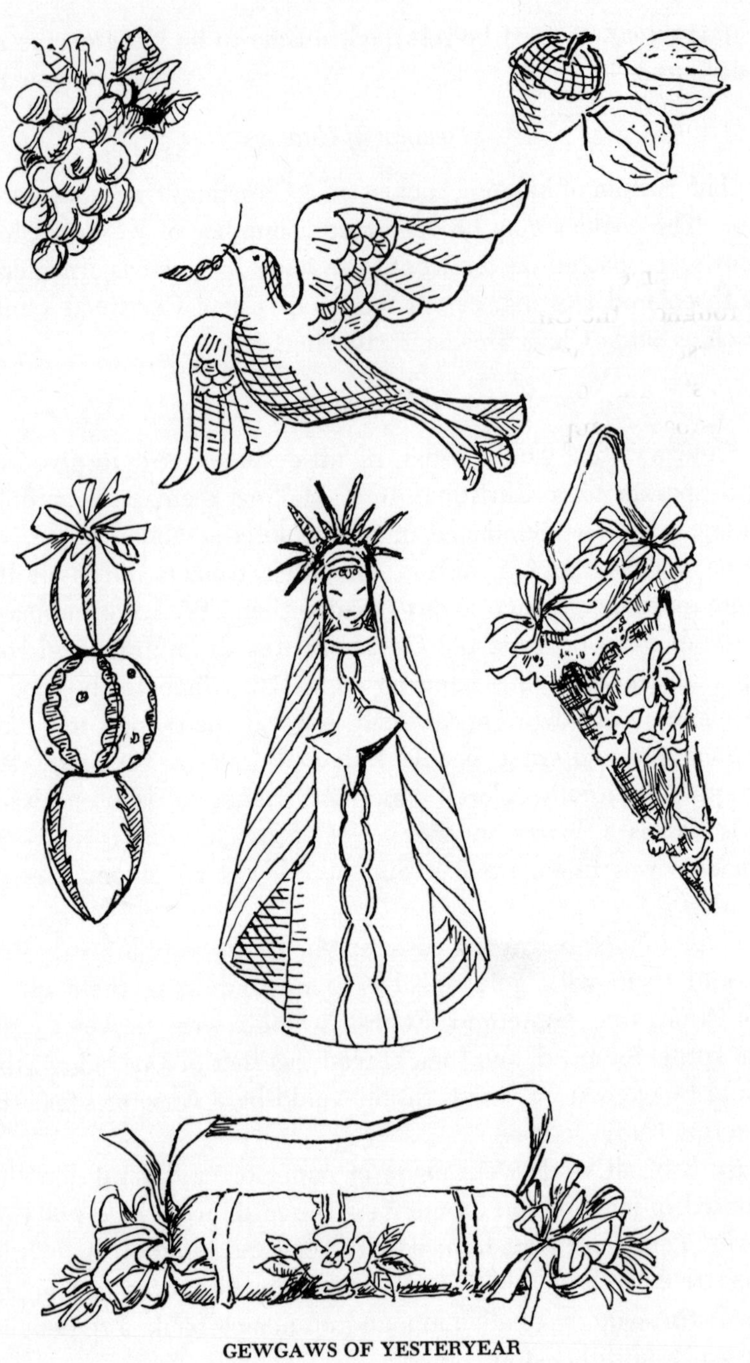

GEWGAWS OF YESTERYEAR

Candy canes and ribbon candy make us recall Christmases of our childhood, and even today no tree is completely decorated without the red-and-white-striped candy cane.

TWO CHRISTMAS RECIPES

Hot Mulled Punch

This time-tested recipe from Williamsburg, Virginia, is served throughout the Christmas season:

First of all, you must make a wassail base which, in general, consists of a bowl of choicest ale, flavored with spices and sugar, with roasted apples floating on it after it has been heated. To the wassail base add:

Twelve fat cloves—one for each month of the year
The rind of a lemon
Twelve broken bits of whole cinnamon
Two tablespoons of lump or whole sugar

Place all this in the liquid and let it steep slowly over a simmering flame, never coming to a boil. Serve steaming hot.

English Plum Pudding

Whatever is the main course of your Christmas dinner—turkey, goose or ham, a plum pudding has become well established as the fitting dessert:

Mix 1 pound of chopped suet, ½ pound of brown sugar, ¾ pound of stale bread crumbs, and ¼ pound of flour. Add 5 eggs, 1 teacupful of sweet cider, the juice and grated rind of 1 lemon, 1 pound of currants, 1 pound of raisins, ½ pound of minced candied orange

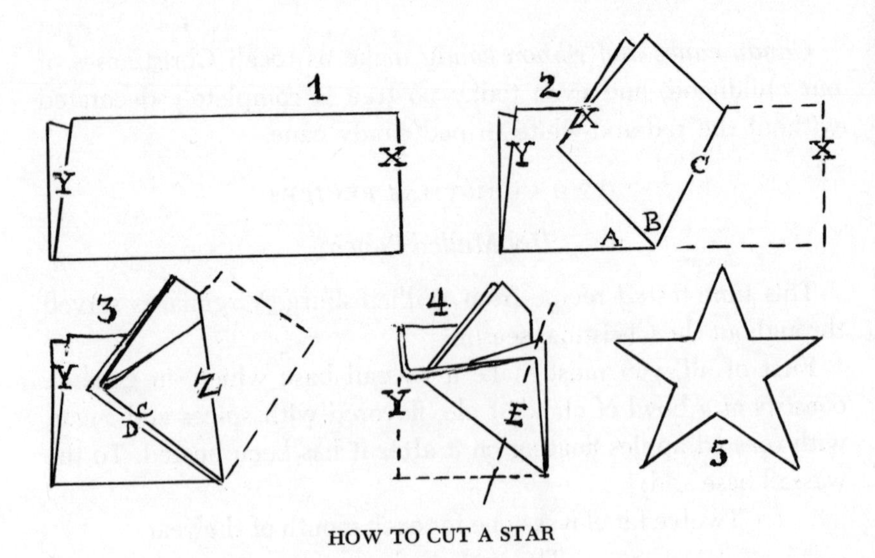

HOW TO CUT A STAR

peel, and about half of a grated nutmeg. When well blended, turn the mixture into a buttered mold with a cover and steam it for seven or eight hours. Garnish with holly and serve with hard sauce.

We are reminded of the lamenting of a flower vendor in London in 1870 about how hard it was to supply enough holly for the Christmas season. The men had to walk miles into the country to find the trees, and the branches were hauled to the city in carts and wagons. He figured 400,000 plum puddings would be served on Christmas Day, and "what Londoner would serve a pudding without a spring of holly on top!"